SUNSHINE GERMAN PHRASE

BY
JOSEPH ROSENBERG

PAPERFRONTS
Elliot Right Way Books
Kingswood, Surrey, U.K.

Copyright notice

© Elliot Right Way Books MCMLXXIII

Partly based on German in 39 Steps, by J. Rosenbery © MCMLXV

Re-issued MCMLXXXV

All rights reserved. No part of this book may be reproduced, stored in a retrieval system, or transmitted, in any form or by any means, electronic, photocopying, mechanical, recording or otherwise, without the prior permission of the copyright owner.

Conditions of sale

This book shall only be sold, lent or hired for profit, trade, or otherwise in its original binding, except where special permission has been granted by the Publishers.

Every effort is made to ensure that Paperfronts and Right Way Books are accurate, and that the information given in them is correct. However, information can become out of date, and author's or printers' errors can creep in. This book is sold, therefore, on the condition that neither Author nor Publisher can be held legally resonsible for the consequences of any error or omission there may be.

**Made and Printed in Great Britain by
Hunt Barnard Printing Ltd., Aylesbury, Bucks.**

CONTENTS

Preface	6
How to Use this Book	7
German Pronunciation	9
German Grammar	15

PART I

Greetings and Leave-Taking	35
Thanks and Apologies	37
'Yes' and Approval	39
'No' and Disapproval	41
Hesitation and Doubt	43
Commands and Requests	45
Questions and Answers	47

CONTENTS

Question Words	49
Enquiry and Information	55
Wants, Wishes, Likes and Dislikes	57
Permission and Necessity	60
Possessives	62
Exclamations	64
Polite Expressions	66
Pronouns	69
'To Have' and 'To Be'	73
Numbers, Date and Time	78
Weights and Measures	86
Notices	88

PART II

Travel	93
Accommodation	114
Taking a Furnished Room	119
Asking the Way	121

CONTENTS

Shops and Shopping	124
The Post Office and Telephone	141
Eating and Drinking	143
Money	157
The Weather and Thermometer	159
Town and Country	162
At the Seaside	166
The Family	168
The Human Body	171
Sport, Amusements, Pastimes	176
Letter Writing	187
Appendix: Countries, their Languages and Inhabitants	213

HOW TO GET HELP IN EMERGENCY.　　　PAGE 218

PREFACE

This book is intended to give a practical knowledge of conversational German, and the phrases chosen should enable visitors to German-speaking countries to express their everyday requirements.

Special attention has been paid to analysing the needs of tourist, holiday-maker and businessman. A feature of the book is the success that has been achieved in including every phrase likely to be needed by the traveller, while still featuring handy pocket size and great ease of reference.

At the very end of the book is a quick-reference section showing how to get help in the event of emergency.

HOW TO USE THIS BOOK

The correct use of a foreign language derives from habit rather than from knowledge. A person could know all the rules of German Grammar, yet still be unable to speak German.

The right way to learn to speak a foreign language is to memorise the most useful words and phrases which occur over and over again. These have been arranged in Part 1 of this book by an experienced language teacher. You have got to know these, so *learn them by heart through constant repetition*.

The second part of the book gives classified lists of useful vocabulary. Words closely related in sense have been grouped together under convenient headings to enable easy reference. The grouping of words in a logical rather than an alphabetical order has been found more suitable for beginners.

There is no need to learn all the words in the second part by heart. They can be looked up when needed and combined with the phrases given in Part 1. Thus the student who was memorising the German for 'I would like to . . .', 'Would you like to?', 'Where can I find . . .?', 'Please show me . . .', etc., has a stock of correct language forms at his command which he can enlarge as occasion arises from the lists provided in the second part of the book. He can further extend his vocabulary by use of a good dictionary.

GERMAN PRONUNCIATION

1. Die Butter ist gut.
2. Die Milch ist warm.
3. Das Wasser ist kalt.
4. Der Mann ist alt.
5. Der Onkel trinkt Bier.

It is not difficult to recognise these sentences as meaning:

1. The butter is good.
2. The milk is warm.
3. The water is cold.
4. The man is old.
5. The uncle drinks beer.

Some words like butter and warm are identical in both languages. Others, although spelt differently, are so similar that they can be easily recognised. But even those words that are spelt alike are pronounced differently, *e.g.* the 'u' in Butter is not pronounced as in the English word *butter*, but as in the English words *put* or *butcher*. German 'w' is pronounced like English 'v' and the rest of the German word *warm* like the English word *arm*.

It is not difficult at all to learn German pronunciation, as – unlike English – it follows simple and straightforward rules which, once mastered, give clear indications as to the correct pronunciation of every German word.

German words are pronounced as they are spelt, *i.e.* each letter and each combination of letters stand for one sound only (not as in English where the same letter may have different sounds, *e.g.* the 'a' in *cat*, *car*, *call* and *cake*). Once the few simple rules given below are mastered, it will be possible to pronounce every German word correctly. German is spoken with more emphasis than English and there is less slurring of syllables. Take for instance the word *General*, which is common to both languages. In German it is a word of three syllables, which in spoken English is almost reduced to one. In German the three syllables are distinctly pronounced: Ge - ne - ral. There are no silent letters with the exception of 'h' when followed by a consonant. Thus the 'k' in Knie is distinctly sounded and so is the 'p' in *Psychiatrie*.

GERMAN PRONUNCIATION

Usually the first syllable is stressed more heavily than the others. But in words beginning with be-, ge-, er-, ver-, zer-, the stress is on the second syllable. Many foreign words retain the stress of their original pronunciation and are pronounced as in their original language, e.g. *Café* and *Restaurant* are pronounced as in French, *Hotel*, *Jockey*, *Beefsteak*, as in English.

The Vowels

Vowels are either long or short. They are short when followed by two or more consonants, otherwise they are long.

- a Long as in *bar*, short like the *u* in *but*
- e Long like the *a* in *gate*, short as in *bet*
- i Always short as in *tin*
- o Long as in *note*, short as in *not*
- u Long as in *rude*, short as in *put*

Modified Vowels

- ä Long like *a* in *gate*; short like *e* in *bet*
- ü Short like the *ir* in *sir*; pronounced with rounded lips

ü Long like the *ee* in *see* (said with rounded lips);

Combination of Vowels
aa, ee, oo Same as *a*, *e*, *o*, but always long
ie, ih Like *ie* in *field*
ei, ai Like *ei* in *height*
au Like *ou* in *house*
eu, äu Like *oi* in *oil*

The Consonants
- b as in English. At the end of a word like *p*
- c Usually like *k*. Before *e* or *i* like *ts* in *nuts*
- d As in English. At the end of a word like *t*
- f As in English
- g As in *go*. At the end of a word like *k*, except in the ending *-ig*, where it sounds like *ich* (see below)
- h before a vowel as in English, otherwise silent
- j like *y* in yes
- k as in English

GERMAN PRONUNCIATION

- l   as in *lamp* (never as in *all*)
- m as in English
- n as in English
- p as in English
- q only occurs in the combination *qu* which is sounded as in *quality*
- r always pronounced fully with the sound we make when gargling
- s as in *rose* before and between vowels, otherwise as in *son*
- t as in English
- v usually like *f*; in many foreign words like English *v*, *e.g.* Violine, Visite, Villa, nervös
- x as in English
- z like *ts* in *its*

- ch after *a, o, u, au* as in *Scotch loch*. Otherwise like *h* in *huge*
- chs like *x*
- sch like *sh* in *ship*
- sp like *shp* at the beginning of a syllable
- st like *sht* at the beginning of a syllable

th like *t*

β is always pronounced like sharp s. It is a special sign to indicate that the preceding vowel is long, *e.g.* to distinguish the long *a* in Straβe from the short *a* in Wasser. At the end of a word β is always used instead of ss. But in a plural word, *ss* is always used.

GERMAN GRAMMAR

Gender

Every noun in German is either masculine, feminine or neuter and the gender is usually indicated by the word preceding the noun. This may be the definite article *der*, *die*, *das*, or other words with three different forms for masculine, feminine and neuter, such as *dieser*, *diese*, *dieses* (this); *jener*, *jene*, *jenes* (that); *jeder*, *jede*, *jedes* (each); *welcher*, *welche*, *welches* (which). The plural is the same as the feminine form in singular i.e. *die* (the), *diese* (these), *jene* (those), etc., but the noun in plural takes various endings according to the gender of the noun *i.e.* most masculine add -*e* in plural, most feminine either -*n* or -*en*, and most neuters of one syllable -*e*. Another change which occurs in the plural is the modification of *a*, *o*, *u* and *au* (see the notes on pronunciation), but this only applies to the masculines adding -*e* and the neuters adding -*er*, not to the feminines adding (-*e*)*n* and those neuters which add -*e*.

Examples:

Singular	Plural	
der Stuhl	die Stühle	the chair(s)
der Schrank	die Schränke	the cupboard(s)
das Haus	die Häuser	the house(s)
das Dach	die Dächer	the roof(s)

but with no modification

die Fahne	die Fahnen	the flag(s)
die Zeitung	die Zeitungen	the newspaper(s)
das Jahr	die Jahre	the year(s)
das Papier	die Papiere	the paper(s)

There are, however, many exceptions to the above rules, *e.g.* masculine nouns ending in *-e* but not modifying, *der Schuh, die Schuhe,* shoe(s), feminines ending in *-e* and modifying, *die Kuh, die Kühe,* cow(s), neuters ending in *-en das Bett, die Betten* bed(s) and others.

Masculine and neuter nouns ending in *-er, -el, -en* or with the endings *-chen* or *-lein* have no plural endings but most of them modify *a, o, u* and *au*.

GERMAN GRAMMAR

In our vocabulary the plural of nouns is indicated like this: *das Buch*, *¨er*, *i.e.* showing both the ending to be added and any modification to be applied to a vowel.

The indefinite article is *ein* for both masculine and neuter, and *eine* for the feminine. Other words like it are *kein(e)* no; *mein(e)* my; *dein(e)* your; *sein(e)* his; *ihr(e)* her; *unser(e)* our; *Ihr(e)* your.

The plurals are the same as the feminine singular; *keine*; *meine*; *deine*; etc. Although words preceded by *ein* (or *kein*, or *mein* etc.) may be either masculine or neuter, an adjective between them and the noun indicates the gender of the noun by its ending: *ein guter Tag*, a good day shows by the *-er* ending that *Tag* is masculine, and *ein gutes Kind* by the *-es* ending that *Kind* is neuter.

Adjectives preceding a feminine noun end in *-e* (*eine gute Suppe*, a good soup) and so do all adjectives preceded by *der, die, das* or any of the similar words mentioned above. In plural adjectives end in *-en*, irrespective of whether they are preceded by one of the words of the *der, die, das* or the *ein, eine* group, but if no word from either group precedes the adjective, it ends in *e*.

Examples:

die braunen Schuhe,	the brown shoes
meine braunen Schuhe,	my brown shoes
drei kleine Kinder,	three little children

Gender

Although there are no rules which cover all words, the following will be found useful.

Masculine are:

Names of males, stones, days, month, seasons.

Feminine are:
 (*a*) Names of female beings (except those ending in -chen and -lein).
 (*b*) Most words ending in -e, except male beings.
 (*c*) Words ending in -ei, -heit, -keit, -ung, -schaft, -in.
 (*d*) Words of foreign origin ending in -ion, -ie, -ik, -tät.

Neuter are:
 (*a*) Words ending in -chen and -lein. Either of these endings may be added to any noun to form a diminutive.

GERMAN GRAMMAR

(b) The Infinitive when used as a noun (das Essen).
(c) Names of metals, countries, towns, except die Schweiz (Switzerland), die Türkei, die Tschechoslovakei, die Vereinigten Staaten (U.S.A.).
(d) Most nouns with the prefix Ge-.

Note: A compound noun has the gender of its last part, e.g.
das Blei + der Stift = der Bleistift (pencil).
die Hand + der Schuh = der Handschuh (glove).
das Streichholz + die Schachtel = die Streichholzschachtel (match box).

Declensions

Both the definite articles and the indefinite articles (and the words similar to them) are declined according to the function of the noun. If the noun is the direct object in a sentence (the *accusative case*) the masculine singular form of the article is the only one that changes. In the possessive (or *genitive*) case the masculine and neuter forms are the same, and so are the feminine forms, singular and the plural. In the case of the indirect object (*the dative case*) the masculine and the neuter singulars are the same, but feminine singular is the different from the plural.

but feminine singular is the different from the plural.

	masc.	fem.	neut.	Plural
Nominative:	der	die	das	die
Accusative:	den	die	das	die
Genitive:	des	der	des	der
Dative:	dem	der	dem	den

Singular ... *Plural*

In the genitive case, the noun takes the ending *-s* (*-es* in words of one syllable) in both masculine and neuter, and the ending *-n* in the dative plural.

In the sentence *Der Vater des Kindes schreibt dem Lehrer einen Brief.* The father of the child writes the teacher a letter.

der Vater is in the Nominative, because it is the subject of the sentence.
des Kindes is in the Genitive, because it indicates possession
einen Brief is in the Accusative, because it indicates the direct object
dem Lehrer is in the Dative, because it is the indirect object.

The indefinite article (and all similar words) are declined in the same way.

Adjectives used in connection with the genitive or dative case (irrespec-

GERMAN GRAMMAR

tive of whether preceded by a word of the *der, die, das* or *ein, eine* group) end in *-en*.

The adjective preceding a masculine noun in the accusative singular also ends in *-en* e.g. *ich habe einen neuen Hut* I have a new hat.

Comparisons

To form the comparative of adjectives add *-er* and to form the superlative *-ste*.

groß, big   größer, bigger   der (die, das) grßöte, the biggest
gut, good   besser, better   der (die, das) beste, the best

Note that *a, o, u* and *au* take the Umlaut in both the comparative and superlative and also the irregular forms of *gut*.

Conjugations

The infinitive of verbs, with the few exceptions, ends in *-en* e.g. *sagen*, to say.

Exceptions:
    sein, to be   tun, to do

By cutting off the *-en* (or *n*) ending, the stem of the verb is derived, to which endings are added in accordance with the following pattern:

Present tense

	Singular	Plural
1st person:	ich ... e	wir ... en
2nd person:	du ... st	ihr ... t
3rd person:	(er sie, es) ... t	sie ... en

The form with *du* is used when talking to a child, relative or good friend, and the form with *ihr* to two or more; adults who are not relatives or intimate friends, are addressed as *Sie* with the verb ending in *-en*. Thus 'are you coming' may be translated *Kommst du? Kommt ihr?* or *Kommen Sie?* according to whom the question is addressed.

Note that in forming questions the order of words is reversed.

Some verbs have slight modification in the 2nd and 3rd person singular:

schlafen, to sleep: ich schlafe, du schläfst, er schläft
lesen, to read: ich lese, du liest, er liest
sehen, to see: ich sehe, du siehst, er sieht
nehmen, to take: ich nehme, du nimmst, er nimmt
essen, to eat: ich esse, du ißt, er ißt

A few verbs drop the final -e in the 1st and 3rd person singular

GERMAN GRAMMAR

wissen, to know: ich weiß, du weißt, er weiß
können, to be able: ich kann, du kannst, er kann
wollen, to want: ich will, du willst, er will
müssen, to have to: ich muß, du mußt, er muß

The Imperative

The Imperative (expressing a command or request) is derived from the present tense and has three forms according to whether one addresses children and intimates in either singular or plural, or adults with whom one is not on familiar terms:

	Familiar Form		Polite Form
Come	*Sing.* Komm!	*Pl.* Kommt!	Kommen Sie!
Drink	Trink!	Trinkt!	Trinken Sie!
Eat	Iß!	Eßt!	Essen Sie!

As in English, the Imperative is usually replaced in polite conversation by such expressions as:

Would you please ... Würden Sie bitte ...
Would you be kind enough ... Würden Sie so freundlich sein ...
Could you please ... Könnten Sie bitte ...

The Imperfect

The Imperfect, which expresses descriptions in the past, has the following endings in all regular verbs:

	Singular	Plural
1st person:	ich ... te	wir ... ten
2nd person:	du ... test	ihr ... tet
3rd person:	er (sie, es) ... te	sie ... ten

Irregular, also called strong verbs change their root vowel and omit the *te* syllable in singular and the *t* in plural:

ich kam, I came **ich sah,** I saw **ich war,** I was **ich nahm,** I took

The Perfect

Most happenings in the past, especially in conversation, are expressed by the perfect. The perfect is a compound verb, consisting of an auxiliary verb (usually *haben*, to have; sometimes *sein* to be) and the past participle, which has the prefix *ge-* and the ending *-t*:

ich habe gefragt, I have asked
Haben Sie das gehört? Did you hear that?

GERMAN GRAMMAR

	Singular	*Plural*
1st person:	ich habe ge...t	wir haben ge...t
2nd person:	du hast ge...t	ihr habt ge...t
3rd person:	er hat ge...t	sie haben ge...t

Verbs with prefixes *be-, ge-, er-, ver-, zer-* form past participles without ge-;

besucht, visited	gehört, belonged
erzählt, told	versucht, tried
zerstört, destroyed	

Strong (irregular) verbs end in *-en*:

gekommen, come	gesehen, seen
geschrieben, written	gegessen, eaten
gegeben, given	

The following verbs form their perfect with *sein*, to be (ich bin, du bist, er ist, wir sind, ihr seid, sie sind):

	Infinitive	Imperfect	Part Participle
To go	gehen	ging	gegangen
to come	kommen	kam	gekommen
to climb	steigen	stieg	gestiegen
to run	laufen	lief	gelaufen
to stay	bleiben	blieb	geblieben
to travel	reisen	reiste	gereist
to drive	fahren	fuhr	gefahren
to ride	reiten	ritt	geritten
to be	sein	war	gewesen
to become	werden	wurde	geworden

Also verbs derived from the above *e.g.*

fortgehen, to go away	ankommen, to arrive
abreisen, to depart	einsteigen, to get in
austeigen, to get out	umsteigen, to change

Separable Verbs

Verbs like *fortgehen*, to go away; *aufstehen*, to get up; *eintreten*, to come in, which consist of two words joined together, are called separable

GERMAN GRAMMAR

verbs. They are separated in the Present tense, in the Imperfect and in the Imperative, but they are joined together in the Infinitive and in the past participle.

The present tense of the above verbs are: *ich gehe ... fort, ich stehe ... auf, ich trete ... ein*. The separated part goes to the end of the sentence and other parts of the sentence in between e.g. *Ich stehe um sechs Uhr auf*, I get up at six o'clock.

The corresponding imperatives are in the polite form:

Gehen Sie fort! Stehen Sie auf! Treten Sie ein!

The past participles are:

fortgegangen, aufgestanden, eingetreten

The Future

The future is a compound tense formed by the auxiliary *werden* and the infinitive:

	Singular	*Plural*
1st person:	ich werde ... en	wir werden ... en
2nd person:	du wirst ... en	ihr werdet ... en
3rd person:	er wird ... en	sie werden ... en

The order of words

Comparison of the German phrases with their English translations will show that the order of words in a German sentence is not the same as in English. The following basic rules will help you to compose German sentences in their correct order:

1. The verb always comes second in a sentence, except in questions, commands and exclamations.

Wir kommen bald wieder	We soon come back
Meine Frau und meine Kinder trinken nicht Kaffee	My wife and my children don't drink coffee.

   Note from the last example that the verb is not necessarily the second word in the sentence, it is the second part of the sentence.

2. When the verb has a compound form (as in the perfect or in the future) the infinitive or past participle is at the end of the sentence and the auxiliary takes the second place.

Am Mittwoch werden wir ins Theater gehen	On Wednesday we shall go to the theatre

Gestern hat es den ganzen Tag geregnet	Yesterday it rained the whole day

3. In a subordinate clause the verb or the auxiliary is at the end.

Sie kann nicht kommen, weil sie sich nicht wohl fühlt	She cannot come because she does not feel well
es regnen wird	it will rain

As in English, this last sentence can also be expressed by starting with 'if it rains, we . . .' In German this would be *Wenn es regnen wird, werden wir nicht gehen*: *i.e.* if you start with the dependent clause, the whole of it counts as the first part so that the verb must immediately follow (see No. 1 above).

4. If the verb is negative *nicht* follows the verb, but it precedes an infinitive or a past participle.

Ich gehe nicht	I am not going
Er ist gestern nicht gekommen	He did not come yesterday
Wir werden morgen nicht spielen	We shall not play tomorrow.

5. If any other part of the sentence is negative *nicht* precedes it.

Sie ist nicht zu Hause	She is not at home
Wir werden nicht zum Mittagessen zurück sein	We shall not be back for lunch.

Note the use of kein(e) for *not a*:

Ich habe kein Messer (keine Gabel), I haven't got a knife (fork).

Further study

To cover other parts of grammar would be beyond the scope of this book, but we can recommend the following three books by Joseph Harvard published by the University of London Press:

1. *Beginner's German* which clearly explains the elements of grammar to a student learning without a teacher.

2. *Conversational German* which in addition to systematic fluency practice contains a complete reference grammar.

3. *German for Pleasure* which introduces the student to the reading of stories, songs, plays and dialogues of German films.

GERMAN GRAMMAR

The Alphabet

Roman type is now used everywhere in German-speaking countries, but occasionally shop sign and street names are still indicated in Gothic type. As all German books and newspapers are now printed in Roman type, this book follows the general practice and the Gothic characters are given here for reference only.

A	𝔄	a	ah	H	ℌ	h	hah
B	𝔅	b	bay	I	ℑ	i	ee
C	ℭ	c	tsay	J	ℑ	j	yot
D	𝔇	d	day	K	𝔎	k	kah
E	𝔈	e	ay	L	𝔏	l	ell
F	𝔉	f	eff	M	𝔐	m	emm
G	𝔊	g	gay	N	𝔑	n	enn

O	𝔒	o	oh	U	𝔘	u	oo
P	𝔓	p	pay	V	𝔙	v	fow
Q	𝔔	q	koo	W	𝔚	w	vay
R	𝔑	r	err	X	𝔛	x	iks
S	𝔊	ſ	ess	Y	𝔜	y	ip-see-lon
T	𝔗	t	tay	Z	𝔷	z	tset

ch ch   ck ck   sz ß   tz tz

Part 1

GREETINGS AND LEAVE-TAKING

Guten Morgen!	Good morning
Guten Tag!	Good day
Guten Abend!	Good evening
Gute Nacht!	Good night
Auf Wiedersehen!	Good bye
Bis später!	See you later
Bis morgen!	See you tomorrow
Gute Reise!	Good journey
Viel Glück!	Good luck
Schlafen Sie wohl!	Sleep well
Gute Besserung!	Speedy recovery

Grüßen sie bitte | Ihren Herrn Vater (Gemahl) | Kind regards to | your father (husband)
 | Ihre Frau Mutter (Gemahlin) | | your mother (wife)

Ihr Fräulein Tochter	your daughter

The latter are, of course, very formal and polite and with nearer acquaintance the Herrn, Frau, Fräulein are omitted or replaced by Christian names. There is no equivalent to English *sir* (*mein Herr* is only used by waiters and Hotel staff but a married woman may be addressed as *gnädige Frau* and an unmarried woman as *gnädiges Fräulein*). If you know a person's rank or profession these may be added to the greeting, *e.g.*

Guten Morgen, Herr Doktor. Guten Tag Herr Hauptman (captain). Guten Abend, Frau Professor.

THANKS AND APOLOGIES

Danke. Danke schön	Thanks. Thank you
Vielen Dank	Thank you very much
Das ist sehr freundlich von Ihnen	It's very kind of you
Keine Ursache	Don't mention it
Gestatten Sie bitte	Allow me
Bitte sehr	Please do. (Also said when giving something, offering one's seat, letting someone pass, etc.)
Verzeihung. Entschuldigen Sie	Sorry. Excuse me
Ich bitte um Entschuldigung	I beg your pardon
Ich bitte vielmals um Entschuldigung	I apologize
Es tut mir sehr leid	I am very sorry

Wie bitte?	I beg your pardon? (When meaning "I did not quite catch what you said")
Es tut mir leid, daß ich Sie warten ließ	I am very sorry to have kept you waiting
Das macht nichts	That doesn't matter
Ich habe mich leider verspätet	I'm sorry I'm late
Ich konnte nicht früher herkommen	I couldn't get here before

'YES' AND APPROVAL

Ja. Jawohl	Yes. Indeed
Gewiß	Certainly
Selbstverständlich} Natürlich}	Of course
Ganz recht} sehr richtig}	Quite right
Gut. Schön	All right
Na schön	Very well (reluctant agreement)
Sie haben recht	You are right
Ich bin sehr dafür	I am all for it
Ich bin einverstanden	I agree
Fraglos. Ohne Frage	Without question
Zweifellos. Ohne Zweifel	Without doubt
Nett. Hübsch. Schön	Nice. Pretty. Beautiful

Ausgezeichnet. Wunderbar. Großartig	Excellent. Wonderful. Magnificent
Es (er, sie) gefällt mir	I like it (him, her)
Sie gefallen mir	I like them
Er (sie) ist | sehr sympathisch	He (she) is very nice
Sie sind	They are

'NO' AND DISAPPROVAL

Aber nein	Oh no
Auf keinen Fall	Not in the least
Ich glaube nicht	I don't think so
Gewiß nicht	Certainly not
Noch nicht	Not yet
Durchaus nicht	Not at all
Es hat keinen Zweck	It's no good
Es macht nichts	Never mind
Es spielt keine Rolle	It doesn't matter
Es macht keine Umstände	It's no trouble
Ich habe nichts dagegen	I don't mind
Ich weiß nicht	I don't know
Im Gegenteil	On the contrary
Ich bin nicht ganz mit Ihnen einverstanden	I don't agree with you

Ich glaube nicht, daß Sie damit recht haben	I don't think you are right there
Da bin ich anderer Meinung	That's where I disagree with you
Ich kann es Ihnen leider nicht sagen	I am afraid I can't tell you
Ich habe nicht die geringste Ahnung	I haven't the slightest idea
Es ist ganz unmöglich	It's quite impossible
Es kommt gar nicht in Frage	It's out of the question
Es ist mir ganz unmöglich	I couldn't possibly do it
Es ist höchst unwahrscheinlich	It's most unlikely
Ich glaube es nicht	I don't believe it
Ich kann es nicht glauben	I can't believe it
Ich glaube nicht ein Wort davon	I don't believe a word of it
Unsinn!	What nonsense!
Es (er, sie) gefällt mir nicht	I don't like it (him, her)
Es ist ganz abscheulich	It's really awful
Es ist ekelhaft. Widerlich	It is nasty. Disgusting
Ich kann ihn nicht ausstehen	I can't stand him
Ein höchst unangenehmer Mensch	A most unpleasant sort of person
Er ist mir nicht gerade sympathisch	I can't say I like him

HESITATION AND DOUBT

Vielleicht	Perhaps
Man kann nie wissen	One never can tell
Das ist schwer zu sagen	That's hard to tell
Ich bin nicht ganz sicher	I'm not quite sure
Schon möglich	Perhaps so
Höchst wahrscheinlich	Very likely
So scheint's	It seems so
Das ist anzunehmen	I suppose so
So sagt man	People say so
Mag sein	Maybe
Glauben Sie wirklich?	Do you really think so?
Es ist durchaus möglich	It's quite possible
Wahrscheinlich	Probably
Es würde mich nicht überraschen	I shouldn't be surprised
Es ist höchst unwahrscheinlich	It's most improbable

Ich halte es kaum für möglich	I hardly think it possible
Er ist wahrscheinlich nicht zu Hause	He's probably not in
Er könnte dort sein	He might be there
Ich glaube nicht, daß sie kommen wird	I don't think she will come
Ich nehme an, daß er's tun wird	I expect he will do it
Ich bezweifele, ob er's tun wird	I doubt whether he will do it
Ich bezweifele es stark	I very much doubt it
Ich glaube, Sie irren sich	I am afraid you may be mistaken
Sind Sie dessen ganz sicher?	Are you quite sure of it?
Es kommt darauf an	That depends
Das ist Ansichtssache	That's a matter of opinion
Das ist Geschmacksache	It's a matter of taste
Ich mache mir nicht viel aus solchen Sachen	I don't quite care for that sort of thing
Solche Menschen sind mir nicht sonderlich sympathisch	I don't much care for that sort of person
Das ist alles sehr schön und gut, aber ...	That's all very well, but ...

COMMANDS AND REQUESTS

To turn an order into a polite request, you may say 'bitte' either before or after the following imperatives:

Kommen Sie! Warten Sie!	Come. Wait
Bitte kommen sie	Please come
Schreiben Sie! Lesen Sie!	Write. Read
Kommen Sie her!	Come here
Kommen Sie herein!	Come in
Kommen Sie herauf!	Come up
Kommen Sie schnell!	Come quickly
Sprechen Sie Englisch!	Speak English
Sprechen Sie langsam!	Speak slowly
Sprechen Sie nicht so schnell!	Don't speak so fast
Sprechen Sie lauter!	Speak louder

Fahren Sie schneller!	Drive faster
Fahren Sie nicht so schnell!	Don't drive so fast
Nicht so schnell (langsam)	Not so fast (slow)
Kommen Sie jetzt nicht herein	Don't come in now
Gehen Sie da nicht hinein	Don't go in there
Warten Sie nicht	Don't wait
Nehmen Sie das nicht	Don't take that
Nehmen Sie Platz	Take a seat
Bringen Sie mir (uns) ...	Bring me (us) ...
Ich möchte ...	I should like ...
Könnte ich ... haben?	Could I have ... ?
Würden Sie so gut sein	Would you be so kind as to
mir ein Glas Wasser bringen	bring me a glass of water
mir Feuer geben	give me a light
dies reparieren	to repair that
dies reparieren lassen	to have this repaired
das Fenster schliessen	shut the window

QUESTIONS AND ANSWERS

Sie kommen, nicht wahr?	You are coming, aren't you?
Sie warten, nicht wahr?	You are waiting, aren't you?
Sie verstehen, nicht wahr?	You understand, don't you?
Sie sprechen Englisch, nicht wahr?	You speak English, don't you?
Es ist heute Dienstag, nicht wahr?	It's Tuesday today, isn't it?
Das ist genug, nicht wahr?	That's enough, isn't it?
Kommen Sie?	Are you coming?
Warten Sie?	Are you waiting?
Rauchen Sie?	Do you smoke?
Sprechen Sie Englisch?	Do you speak English
Kommt Ihr Mann (Ihre Frau)?	Is your husband (your wife) coming?
Trinkt er (sie) Bier?	Does he (she) drink beer?
Was nimmt er (sie)?	What is he (she) having?
Ja, ich komme	Yes, I'm coming

Nein, ich komme nicht	No, I'm not coming
Ja, ich verstehe	Yes, I understand
Nein, ich verstehe nicht	No, I don't understand
Ja, er (sie) kommt	Yes, he (she) is coming
Nein, er (sie) kommt nicht	No, he (she) is not coming
Ja, er (sie) trinkt es	Yes, he (she) drinks it
Nein, er (sie) trinkt es nicht	No, he (she) does not drink it

Note that there is no difference in German between 'I come' and 'I am coming', nor is there between 'Are you coming?' and 'Do you come?' The same applies to the interrogative: 'Rauchen Sie?' is both 'Do you smoke?' and 'Are you smoking?' 'Nicht wahr?' stands for English 'Aren't you? – Don't you? – Haven't you? – Is he? – does she? – Have they? – Can't you? – and the numerous other question tags particular to the English language. "Nicht wahr?" is short for "Ist es nicht wahr?" Isn't it true?

QUESTION WORDS

Where

Wo ist er?	Where is he?
Wo is der Mann?	Where is the man?
Wo ist mein Freund?	Where is my friend?
Wo ist die Frau?	Where is the woman?
Wo ist meine Freundin?	Where is my girl-friend?
Wo sind die Lampen?	Where are the lamps?
Wo sind sie?	Where are they?
Wo sind Sie?	Where are you?
Wo bin ich?	Where am I?
Wo sind wir?	Where are we?
Wo gehen Sie hin?	Where are you going (to)?
Wo kommen Sie her?	Where do you come from?

2. What

Was ist das?	What is that?
Was sagen Sie?	What do you say? *or* What are you saying?
Was tun Sie?	What are you doing?
Was essen Sie?	What are you eating? *or* What do you eat?
Was sagt er?	What does he say? *or* What is he saying?
Was itß sie?	What is she eating? *or* What does she eat?
Was trinken Sie?	What are you drinking? *or* What do you drink?

Note

1. 'What' in the combination 'with what' is **womit**, *e.g.*

Womit schreiben Sie?	What are you writing with?

2. Learn the following expressions where 'what' is translated differently:

QUESTION WORDS

Wieviel Uhr ist es jetzt?	What time is it?
Wie heißen Sie?	What is your name?
Wie heißt dieser Ort?	What is the name of this place?
diese Stadt?	this town?
dieses Dorf?	this village?

3. Who

Wer ist das?	Who's that?
Wer geht da?	Who goes there?
Wer ist dieser Mann?	Who is this man?
Wer ist diese Frau?	Who is this woman?
Wer sind diese Leute?	Who are these people?
Wer weiß das?	Who knows that?
Wer sagt das?	Who says that?

4. Whom, of whom, to whom

Wen sehen Sie?	Whom do you see?
Wen haben Sie gesehen?	Whom have you seen? *or* Whom did you see?

Für wen ist das?	For whom is that?
Wem schreiben Sie?	To whom are you writing?
Wem gehört das?	To whom does this belong?
Mit wem gehen Sie?	With whom do you go?
Von wem sprechen Sie?	Of whom are you speaking?
Von wem haben Sie das?	From whom have you got this?

5. *How much, how many*

Wieviel kostet das?	How much does this cost?
Wieviele Kilometer?	How many kilometres?
Wieviel haben Sie?	How much have you got?
Wieviele hat er?	How many has he got?

6. *How*

Wie lange?	How long?
Wie bitte?	How do you mean?
Wie kommt das?	How's that? What is the reason for it?

QUESTION WORDS

Wie geht's?	How goes it? (How are you)
Wie geht's Ihrem Vater?	How is your father?
Ihrer Mutter?	your mother?
Ihrem Sohn?	your son?
Ihrer Tochter?	your daughter?
Wie geht's den Kindern?	How are the children?
den Eltern?	the parents?

7. *When*

Wann kommt er? — When is he coming?
Wann kommen Sie? — When are you coming?
Wann geht sie? — When is she going?
Wann kann ich Sie wiedersehen? — When can I see you again?

8. *Why*

Warum tun Sie das? — Why do you do that?
Warum sagen Sie das? — Why do you say that?
Warum gehen Sie schon? — Why are you leaving already?
Warum kommen Sie nicht? — Why aren't you coming?
Warum nicht? — Why not?

9. Miscellaneous

Welcher, welche, welches?	Which one?
Wie oft? Wie lange?	How often? How long?
Wie weit? Wozu?	How far? What for?
Was nun?	What next?
Wieviel Uhr ist es?	What's the time?
Der Wievielte ist es?	What's the date?
Um wieviel Uhr?	At what time?
An welchem Tage?	On what day?
In welchem Monat?	In what month?
In welchem Jahr?	In what year?
Was ist los?	What is the matter?
Wozu dient das?	What is this for?
Was gibt es Neues?	What's the news?
Dies oder das?	This one or that one?
So oder so?	Like this or like that?
Wie bitte?	Pardon?

ENQUIRY AND INFORMATION

See also 'Asking One's Way' on p. 67; 'Asking Questions' on pages 34–36

Das Auskunftsbüro
Könnten Sie mir Auskunft geben über
Züge (Schiffe, Flugzeuge) nach ...
Autobusse (Ausflüge) nach ...
die Festspiele (die Austellung) in ...

the inquiry office
Could you give me information about
trains (boats, planes) to ...
buses (excursions) to ...
the festival (the exhibition) at ...

Das Fundbüro
Ich habe ... verloren
Ich habe ... liegen lassen
Im Autobus von ... nach ...

the lost property office
I lost ...
I left behind ...
In the bus from ... to ...

Könnten Sir mir bitte sagen   *Could you please tell me*
wo ich . . . bekommen kann?	where I can get . . . ?
wie dieser Ort heißt?	what this place is called?
was dieses Gebäude ist?	what this building is?
wozu das dient?	what this is for?

Könnten Sie mir bitte   *Could you please*
ein Restaurant empfehlen?	recommend me a restaurant?
einen Hundertmarkschein wechseln?	change a 100 Mark note?
eine Briefmarke verkaufen?	sell me a stamp?
Feuer geben?	give me a light?
Ihre Feder leihen?	lend me your pen?

WANTS, WISHES, LIKES AND DISLIKES

Wollen Sie bitte ...	Will you please ...
Würden Sie bitte ...	Would you please ...
Würden Sie so gut sein ...	Would you be so kind as to ...
Seien Sie so gut ...	Be so kind as to ...
Ich möchte ...	I should like ...
Was wünschen Sie?	What can I do for you?
Was wollen Sie?	What do you want?
Was will er?	What does he want?
Was wollen sie?	What do they want?
Essen Sie gern ...?	Do you like eating ...?
Trinken Sie gern ...?	Do you like drinking ...?
Sehen Sie gern ...?	Do you like seeing ...?
Hören Sie gern ...?	Do you like hearing ...?

Gehen Sie gern ins Theater?	Do you like going to the theatre?
ins Kino?	the cimena?
in die Oper?	the opera?
in den Zirkus?	the circus?
Spielen Sie gern Tennis?	Do you like playing tennis?
Karten?	cards?
Schach?	chess?
Dame?	draughts?
Haben Sie Hunde gern?	Are you fond of dogs?
Katzen	cats?
Rosen	roses?
Tulpen	tulips?
Ja, sehr. Lieber als ...	Yes, very. More than ...
Ganz gern	I like them (or it)
Aber ich ziehe ... vor	But I prefer ...
Aber ich gehe lieber ...	But I would rather go to ...
Ich habe ... nicht gern	I don't like ...
Ich gehe nicht gern ...	I don't like going to ...
Ich spiele ... nicht gern	I don't like playing ...
ich esse ... nicht gern	I don't like eating ..

WANTS, WISHES, LIKES AND DISLIKES

Ich sehe ... nicht gern	I don't like seeing ...
Er (sie, es) gefällt mir	I like him (her, it)
Sie gefallen mir	I like you (them)
Wie hat es Ihnen gefallen?	How did you like it?
Es hat mir sehr (großartig) gefallen	I liked it very much (immensely)
Es hat mir hier (dort) gut gefallen	I liked it here (there)
Er (sie, es) hat mir nicht gefallen	I didn't like him (her, it)
Sie haben mir nicht gefallen	I didn't like you (them)

PERMISSION AND NECESSITY

Kann ich
   diesen Platz haben?
   das dahinlegen?
   da hineingehen?
   eins nehmen?
   das behalten?
Können wir ...?
Gestatten Sie ...

Can (may) I
   have this seat?
   put that there?
   go in there?
   take one?
   keep that?
Can (may) we ...?
Allow me ...

Ist es gestattet (verboten)
   zu rauchen?
   hier zu baden?
   hier durchzugehen?
   da durchzufahren?
   hier zu lagern?

Is it permitted (forbidden)
   to smoke?
   to bathe here?
   to walk through here?
   to drive through there?
   to camp here?

PERMISSION AND NECESSITY

Aber bitte		Please do	
Bitte nicht		Please don't	
Selbstverständlich		By all means	
Keineswegs		By no means	
Muß man	lange warten?	Does one have to	wait long?
Müssen wir	Eintritt zahlen?	Do we have to	pay to go in?
Muß ich	ein Trinkgeld lassen?	Do I have to	leave a tip?
Muß er	dafür bezahlen?	Does he have to	pay for it?
Müssen sie	da hingehen?	Do they have to	go there?

POSSESSIVES

mein Vater	my father
meine Mutter	my mother
meine Eltern	my parents
sein Sohn	his son
seine Tochter	his daughter
ihr Bruder	her brother
ihre Schwester	her sister
Ihr Onkel	your uncle
Ihre Tante	your aunt
unser Haus	our house
unsere Kinder	our children
ihr Vetter	their cousin (male)
ihre Kusine	their cousin (female)
Dies gehört mir	This belongs to me

POSSESSIVES

Sie gehören uns	They belong to us
Gehört das Ihnen?	Does this belong to you?
Gehören sie Ihnen?	Do they belong to you?

EXCLAMATIONS

Was für ein schöner	Hut!	What a beautiful	hat!
	Garten!		garden!
	Sonnenuntergang!		sunset!
Was für eine schöne	Tasche!	What a beautiful	bag!
	Blume!		flower!
	Landschaft!		landscape!
Was für ein schönes	Tier!	What a beautiful	animal!
	Kleid!		dress!
	Gemälde!		painting!
Was für schöne	Bilder!	What beautiful	pictures!
	Blumen!		flowers!
	Bäume!		trees!

EXCLAMATIONS

Was für herrliches (schreckliches) Wetter!	What a lovely (nasty) day!
Achtung!	Mind! Look out!
Vorsicht!	Careful!
Hallo!	Hallo!
Wie schön!	How nice!
Wie schrecklich!	How horrible!
Mein Gott!	Good gracious!
Einen Augenblick bitte!	One moment, please

POLITE EXPRESSIONS

See also 'Greetings and Leave Taking' p. 35; 'Thanks and Apologies' p. 37.

Darf ich vorstellen...	May I introduce...
Sehr angenehm	Pleased to meet you
Wollen Sie mich bitte dem Herrn (der Dame) vorstellen?	Will you please introduce me to the gentleman (to the lady)?
Es freut mich, Ihre Bekanntschaft gemacht zu haben	I am glad to have made your acquaintance
Das Vergnügen ist meinerseits	The pleasure is mine
Ich hoffe, Sie bald wiederzusehen	I hope to see you again soon
Besuchen Sie uns doch am Sonntag	Come to see us on Sunday
Um welche Zeit darf ich kommen?	At what time may I come?
Gegen vier, wenn es Ihnen recht ist	Towards 4 o'clock, if it is convenient to you

POLITE EXPRESSIONS

Es wird mir ein Vergnügen sein	It will be a pleasure
Ich freue mich darauf	I am looking forward to it
Ist ... zu Hause?	Is ... at home?
Ich möchte ... sprechen	I should like to see ...
Wen darf ich melden?	What name shall I say?
Wollen Sie bitte nähertreten	Will you come in please
Wollen Sie bitte Platz nehmen	Will you please take a seat
Wollen Sie bitte einen Augenblick warten	Will you please wait a few moments
Entschuldigen Sie, daß ich Sie warten ließ	I am sorry to have kept you waiting
Entschuldigen Sie meine Verspätung	I am sorry for being late
Störe ich Sie nicht?	Am I not disturbing you?
Nicht im geringsten	Not at all
Womit kann ich Ihnen dienen?	What can I do for you?
Ich bringe Ihnen Grüße von ...	I have come to deliver greetings from ...
Sehr liebenswürdig von Ihnen	Very kind of you
Wie geht es ihm (ihr)?	How is he (she)?

Wie geht es ihnen (Ihnen)?	How are they (you)?
Danke gut. Und Ihnen?	Thanks, fine. And you?
Ganz gut. Ich war krank, aber es geht mir besser	Quite well. I was ill, but I am better now
Das freut mich	I am pleased to hear it
Das tut mir leid	I am sorry to hear it
Kann ich Ihnen etwas anbieten?	May I offer you something?
Danke vielmals. Ich habe aber eben gespeist	Many thanks. But I just had a meal
Ich muß leider gehen	I am sorry I have to go now
Man erwartet mich um . . . Uhr	I am expected at . . . o'clock
Bitte kommen Sie bald wieder	Please come again soon
Mit dem größten Vergnügen	With the greatest of pleasure

PRONOUNS

'Me, Us, You, Him, Her, It, Them'

1. Er erwartet mich (uns, Sie, sie) — He is expecting me (us, you, them)

   Ich kenne ihn (sie, es, dich, Sie) — I know him (her, it, you in the familiar and polite forms)

   Kennen Sie ihn (sie, es, mich, uns)? — Do you know him (her or them, it, me, us)?

   Ich weiß es; Ich weiß es nicht — I know it. I don't know it

   Wissen Sie es (nicht)? — Do you (don't you) know it?

Note that *kennen* means 'to know' in the sense of 'to be acquainted with.' *Wissen* (ich, er, sie, es weiβ; wir, Sie sie wissen means 'to have knowledge of'.

2.
Nehmen Sie meinen Bleistift	Take my pencil
Nehmen Sie ihn. Da ist er	Take it. There it is
Nehmen Sie meine Feder	Take my pen
Nehmen Sie sie. Da ist sie	Take it. There it is
Nehmen Sie mein Buch	Take my book
Nehmen Sie es. Da ist es	Take it. There it is
Da sind meine Streichhölzer	There are my matches
Nehmen Sie sie. Nehmen Sie sie nicht	Take them. Don't take them
Nehmen Sie ihn (sie, es) nicht	Don't take it

As *der Bleistift* is *masculine* and *die Feder* feminine in German, the words for he (*er*) and she (*sie*), him (*ihn*) and her (*sie*) are used when referring to them. Note that *sie* can mean she, her, they or them and, when spelt *Sie*, also 'you'.

To me, to us, to him, to her, to them, to you

Sagen Sie mir	Tell me
Schreiben Sie uns	Write to us

PRONOUNS

Bringen Sie	ihm	Bring	him
Geben Sie	ihr	Give	her
Helfen Sie	ihnen	help	them
Ich kann Ihnen nicht helfen		I cannot help you	
Ich kann es Ihnen nicht sagen		I cannot tell you	

When *me, him, her, them* and *you* are used in the sense of 'to me', 'to him' 'to her', etc. they are *mir, ihm, ihr, ihnen* or *Ihnen* in German, *i.e.* they are the indirect objects and therefore in the dative case (see p. 16). *Helfen*, to help also requires the dative case as it means 'to give assistance to'. Note that *uns* is used for both 'us' and 'to us'.

'Isn't it? Don't you? Aren't you? Isn't he? Doesn't she?' etc.

Sie sind Deutscher, nicht wahr?	You are German, aren't you?
Sie sprechen englisch, nicht wahr?	You speak English, don't you?
Das ist hübsch, nicht wahr?	That's pretty, isn't it?
Sie kommen heute abend, nicht wahr?	You are coming tonight, aren't you?

Er ist Ihr Verlobter, nicht wahr?	He is your fiancé, isn't he?
Sie spricht italienisch, nicht wahr?	She speaks Italian, doesn't she?

Nicht wahr is short for Ist es nicht wahr? Isn't it true?

'There is, there are, that is, these are'

Es ist kein Zimmer frei	There is no room vacant
Es sind keine Stühle da	There are no chairs
Das ist meine ältere Tochter	That is my elder daughter
Das sind meine Kinder	These are my children
Was gibt es zu essen?	What is there to eat?
Gibt es keinen Salat?	Is there no salad?
Es gibt warme Würstchen	There are hot sausages
Was gibt es im Kino?	What is there on at the cinema?
Es gibt einen Film mit ...	There is a film with ...

Note that *es gibt* is used for both 'there is' and 'there are' in the sense of 'it's on the menu or programme', 'it is available'.

'TO HAVE' AND 'TO BE'

haben
ich habe
Sie ⎫
wir ⎬ haben
sie ⎭
er ⎫
sie ⎬ hat
es ⎭
Ich habe Hunger
Ich habe Durst
Ich habe Kopfschmerzen

to have
I have
you ⎫
we ⎬ have
they ⎭
he ⎫
she ⎬ has
it ⎭
I am hungry
I am thirsty
I've got a headache

Sein	*to be*
ich bin	I am
Sie, wir, sie sind	you, we, they are
er, sie, es ist	he, she, it is
Ich bin Engländer*	I am an Englishman
Schotte*	a Scotsman
Amerikaner*	an American
Deutscher	German (man)
Deutsche	German (woman)
Sind Sie Oesterreicher?	are you Austrian (man)?
Oesterreicherin?	Austrian (woman)?
Schweizer?	Swiss (man)?
Schweizerin?	Swiss (women)?

*A woman would say: Engländerin, Schottin, Amerikanerin.

'TO HAVE' AND 'TO BE'

'*No*' *not, don't*

Nein, er ist nicht hier	No, he is not here
Sagen Sie das nicht	Don't say that
Sprechen Sie bitte nicht so schnell	Please don't speak so fast
Warten Sie nicht auf mich (ihn, sie)	Don't wait for me (him, her)
Ich rauche nicht	I don't smoke
Ich habe } kein Messer	I have } no knife
Der Herr hat } keine Gabel	The gentleman has } no fork
Die Dame hat } keinen Löffel	The lady has } no spoon

'No' in the sense of 'not a' is expressed by *kein, keine, kein*, which like *ein, mein*, etc. change to *keinen* in the accusative before a masculine noun in the singular

'*Did you?*' '*I didn't*'

Haben Sie das gehört	Did you hear that?
gesehen?	see
gelesen?	read

geschrieben?	write
gebracht?	bring
Ich habe es nicht gehört (gesehen, etc.)	I didn't hear (see, etc.) it
Haben Sie sich verletzt?	Did you hurt yourself?
geschnitten?	cut
verbrannt?	burn
Ich habe mich verletzt (geschnitten, etc.)	I hurt (cut, etc.) myself
Sind Sie hingegangen?	Did you go there?
früh gekommen?	come early?
lange geblieben?	stay long?
Ich bin nicht hingegangen (früh gekommen, etc.)	I did not go there (come early, etc.)

Haben Sie . . .? is the usual translations for 'did you?'

Sind Sie . . .? is used with verbs denoting moving from one place to another, e.g. *kommen*, to come; *gehen*, to go; *fahren*, to travel, etc.

'TO HAVE' AND 'TO BE'

'I shall...', 'Will you...?'

Ich werde	jetzt essen	I shall	eat now
Wir werden	morgen hingehen	We shall	go there tomorrow
Er wird	es kaufen	He will	buy it
Sie wird	es bezahlen	She will	pay for it
Sie werden	morgen abreisen	They will	leave tomorrow
Werden Sie	wiederkommen?	Will you	come again?
Wird er	zu Fuss gehen?	Will he	go on foot?
Wird sie	das Auto nehmen?	Will she	take the car?
Werden sie	mit der Bahn fahren?	Will they	go by train?

NUMBERS, DATE AND TIME

A Numbers

0	Null	13	dreizehn
1	eins	14	vierzehn
2	zwei	15	fünfzehn
3	drei	16	sechzehn
4	vier	17	siebzehn
5	fünf	18	achtzehn
6	sechs	19	neunzehn
7	sieben	20	zwanzig
8	acht	21	einundzwanzig
9	neun	22	zweiundzwanzig
10	zehn	23	dreiundzwanzig
11	elf	24	vierundzwanzig
12	zwölf	25	fünfundzwanzig

NUMBERS, DATE AND TIME

30	dreißig	80	achtzig
40	vierzig	90	neunzig
50	fünfzig	100	hundert
60	sechzig	200	zweihundert
70	siebzig	1000	tausend

in 1897   im Jahre achtzehnhundertsiebenundneunzig
in 1963   Im Jahre neunzehnhundertdreiundsechzig

B   Ordinal numbers

1st	der (die, das) erste	19th	der neunzehnte
2nd	der zweite	20th	der zwanzigste
3rd	der dritte	21st	der einundzwanzigste
4th	der vierte	100th	der hundertste
5th	der fünfte		

Note. *te* is added to the numbers from 2 to 19, and *-ste* from 20 upwards.

C Days, Months, Seasons

Die Tage	*The days*
Sonntag	Sunday
Montag	Monday
Dienstag	Tuesday
Mittwoch	Wednesday
Donnerstag	Thursday
Freitag	Friday
Sonnabend*	Saturday

*Samstag in Southern Germany, Austria and Switzerland

Die Monate	*The months*
Januar	January
Februar	February
März	March
April	April

NUMBERS, DATE AND TIME

Mai	May
Juni	June
Juli	July
August	August
September	September
Oktober	October
November	November
Dezember	December

Die Jahreszeiten — *The Seasons*

Frühling	Spring
Sommer	Summer
Herbst	Autumn
Winter	Winter

D The Date

Der erste Januar	the 1st of January
der zweite Februar	the 2nd of February

der dritte März	the 3rd of March
der vierte April	the 4th of April
der fünfte Mai	the fifth of May
Der wievielte ist heute?	What is to-day's date?
Heute ist der zwölfte Juni	To-day is the 12th of June

E Divisions of Time

die Sekunde, -n	second
die Minute, -n	minute
die Stunde, -n	hour
eine halbe Stunde	half an hour
eine Viertelstunde	quarter of an hour
der Tag, -e	day
die Nacht, ¨e	night
der Morgen	morning
der Vormittag	forenoon
der Mittag	noon
der Nachmittag	afternoon
der Abend	evening

NUMBERS, DATE AND TIME

die Mitternacht	midnight
morgens	in the morning
mittags	at noon
nachmittags	in the afternoon
nachts	at night
heute	to-day
gestern	yesterday
vorgestern	the day before yesterday
morgen	to-morrow
übermorgen	the day after to-morrow
heute Vormittag	this morning
heute Nachmittag	this afternoon
heute Abend	this evening
heute Nacht	to-night
morgen Vormittag	to-morrow morning
gestern Abend	last night
vor einer Minute (Stunde)	a minute (an hour) ago
vor drei Minuten (Stunden)	3 minutes (hours) ago
vor kurzer Zeit	a little while ago
letzte Woche; letztes Jahr	last week; last year

nächste Woche; nächstes Jahr	next week; next year
früh; spät	early; late
in einer Woche; in vierzehn Tagen	in a week; in a fortnight
manchmal; oft; selten; nie; immer	sometimes; often; seldom; never; always
jeden Tag; jede Woche; jeden Sonntag	every day; every week; every Sunday
einmal; zweimal; dreimal	once; twice; three times

F Telling the Time

Wieviel Uhr ist es?	What time is it?
Es ist drei Uhr	It is three o'clock
Es ist fünf nach drei	It is five past three
Es ist halb vier	It is half past three
Es ist ein Viertel vor vier	It is a quarter to four
Es ist zehn vor vier	It is ten to four
Es ist elf Uhr vormittags	It is eleven a.m.
Es ist zwei Uhr nachmittags	It is two o'clock in the afternoon
Es ist zehn Uhr abends	It is 10 p.m. (in the evening)

NUMBERS, DATE AND TIME

Wecken Sie mich um halb sieben	Call me at half past six
Es ist früh (spät)	It is early; late
die Uhr, -en	*the watch; the clock*
geht richtig (falsch)	is right (wrong)
geht vor (nach)	is fast (slow)
steht	has stopped

WEIGHTS AND MEASURES

Gewicht	*Weight*
ein Kilogramm or Kilo	=1000 Gramm
ein halbes Kilo=ein Pfund	=500 Gramm
hundert Pfund=ein Zentner	
28 Gramm	=1 ounce
453 Gramm	=1 pound
schwer	heavy
leicht	light
wiegen	to weigh
das Gewicht	weight
Übergewicht	overweight
die Waage	scales

WEIGHTS AND MEASURES

Länge	*length*
ein Kilometer	=1000 Meter=$\frac{5}{8}$ of a mile
ein Meter	=100 Zentimeter=39 inches
ein Zentimeter	=10 Millimeter=$\frac{3}{8}$ of an inch
2½ Zentimeter	=1 inch
30 Zentimeter	=1 foot
90 Zentimeter	=1 yard
8 Kilometer	=5 miles

lang, long; **kurz**, short; **weit**, wide; **breit**, broad; **schmal**, narrow; **hoch**, high; **tief**, deep

Inhalt	*Capacity*
ein Liter	=1¾ pints
zwei Liter	=3½ pints
fünf Liter	=1 Gallon ¾ pints
½ Liter (appr.)	=1 pint
1 Liter (appr.)	=1 quart
4½ Liter (appr.)	=1 gallon

NOTICES

Eingang	Entry
Ausgang	Exit
Geöffnet	Open
Geschlossen	Closed
Raucher	Smoker
Nichtraucher	Nonsmoker
Ziehen	Pull
Stoßen	Push
Durchgang verboten	No thoroughfare
Rauchen verboten	No smoking
Eintritt verboten	No entry
Herren	Gentlemen
Damen	Ladies
Besetzt	Engaged
Frei	Vacant

NOTICES

Haltestelle	Stopping Place
Rechts	Right
Links	Left
Zu vermieten	to let
zu verkaufen	for sale
Das Betreten des Rasens ist verboten	Keep off the grass
Vor Taschendieben wird gewarnt	Beware of pickpockets
Hunde sind an der Leine zu führen	Dogs have to be led
Achtung Strassenarbeiten	Road Works Ahead
Kein Zutritt	No Entry (on doors)
Einfahrt verboten	No Entry (on road signs)
Achtung – Lebensgefahr	Danger to life
Zum Meer	To the sea

Part 2

TRAVEL

The Journey	*die Reise, -n*
to travel	reisen
to the seaside	an die See
into the country	aufs Land
to the mountains	ins Gebirge
by train	mit der Eisenbahn
by boat	mit dem Schiff
by air	mit dem Flugzeug
by car	mit dem Auto
on foot	zu Fuß
on a bicycle	mit dem Rad
on a motor-bike	mit dem Motorrad
the journey there	die Hinreise
the journey back	die Rückreise
round trip	die Rundreise

journey round the world	die Weltreise
business trip	die Geschäftsreise
journey abroad	die Auslandsreise
to go abroad	ins Ausland fahren
route	die Route
passport	der Pass, ⸚e
visa	das Visum
tourist agency	das Reisebüro, -s
time-table	der Fahrplan, ⸚e
time of departure	die Abfahrtszeit, -en
time of arrival	die Ankunftszeit, -en
When is the next train (boat, plane) to . . . ?	Wann fährt der nächste Zug (das nächste Schiff, Flugzeug) nach . . .
When do we arrive at . . . ?	Wann kommen wir in . . . an?
booking office	der Fahrkartenschalter, -
ticket	die Fahrkarte, -n
single	einfach
return	hin und zurück
1st class	erster Klasse

TRAVEL

2nd class	zweiter Klasse
season ticket	das Abonnement, -s
platform ticket	die Bahnsteigkarte, -n
valid until	gültig bis . . .
to book a seat	einen Platz reservieren
a berth in the sleeping car	ein Bett im Schlafwagen
a couchette	ein Liegeplatz, ⸚e
to get in	einsteigen
to get out	aussteigen
to change	umsteigen

Luggage — Das Gepäck

porter	der Gepäckträger, -
heavy luggage	das grosse Gepäck
light luggage	das Handgepäck
trunk	der Reisekoffer, -
suitcase	der Handkoffer, -
travelling bag	die Reisetasche, -n
hat-box	die Hutschachtel, -n
rucksack	der Rucksack, ⸚e

attache case	die Aktentasche, -n
to have luggage registered	das Gepäck aufgeben
luggage office	die Gepäckaufgabe
left luggage office	die Gepäckaufbewahrung
luggage receipt	der Gepäckschein
to weigh; weight	wiegen; das Gewicht
overweight	das Übergewicht
to insure	versichern
to send in advance	vorausschicken
to take to the train	zum Zug bringen
to leave in the cloakroom	in der Aufbewahrung lassen
to fetch from the cloakroom	von der Aufbewahrung holen
to pack; to unpack	packen; auspacken

Customs	*der Zoll*
customs office	das Zollamt, ⸚er
customs official	der Zollbeamte, -n
customs examination	die Zollkontrolle, -n
liable to duty	zollpflichtig

TRAVEL

free from duty	zollfrei
to pay duty	Zoll zahlen
to declare	deklarieren
nothing to declare	nichts Zollpflichtiges
something to declare	etwas Zollpflichtiges
for my personal use	für meinen eigenen Gebrauch
... was bought in ...	... wurde in ... gekauft
has been in use for some time	seit einiger Zeit in Gebrauch
the car documents	die Papiere für den Wagen
receipt	die Quittung, -en
passport	der Paß, ⸚sse

Railway   *die Eisenbahn*

(See also section 'Travel', 'Luggage', 'Customs')

station	der Bahnhof, ⸚e
train	der Zug, ⸚e
express through-	der Fernschnellzug
express-	der Schnellzug
fast-	der Eilzug

slow-	der Personenzug
excursion-	der Ausflugszug
railcar	der Triebwagen, -
sleeping car	der Schlafwagen, -
couchette coach	der Liegewagen, -
compartment	das Abteil, -e
smoker, non-smoker	Raucher, Nichtraucher
1st class, 2nd class	erster Klasse, zweiter Klasse
seat; seat reservation	der Platz, ⸚e; die Platzkarte, -n
ticket; bed reservation	die Fahrkarte, -n; die Bettkarte, -
single; return	einfach! hin und zurück
return ticket	die Rückfahrkarte, -n
supplement; -ticket	der Zuschlag; die Zuschlagskarte, -n
booking office	der Schalter, -
to reserve a seat (a bed)	einen Platz (ein Bett) reservieren
corner seat; window-	der Eckplatz, ⸚e; der Fensterplatz, ⸚e
facing the engine	in Fahrtrichtung
back to the engine	entgegengesetzt der Fahrtrichtung

TRAVEL

platform; -ticket	der Bahnsteig, -e; die Bahnsteigkarte, -n
waiting room	der Wartesaal
station master	der Bahnhofsvorsteher
ticket collector	der Schaffner
luggage rack	das Gepäcknetz
For how long is this ticket valid?	Wie lange ist diese Fahrkarte gültig?
Do I have to change?	Muß ich umsteigen?
Does this train connect with the train to...?	Hat dieser Zug Anschluß mit dem nach...?
From which platform (side of the platform) does the 8 o'clock train leave?	Von welchem Bahnsteig (Geleis) fährt der Achtuhrzug?
Please take my handluggage to the train and reserve a seat for me (seats for us)	Bitte bringen Sie das Handgepäck zum Zug und belegen Sie mir einen Platz (uns Plätze)
Is this seat vacant (taken)?	Ist dieser Platz frei (besetzt)?
How long do we stop here?	Wie lange ist hier Aufenthalt?
Do you mind if I open the window?	Haben Sie etwas dagegen, wenn ich das Fenster öffne?

Where can I get a porter?	Wo kann ich einen Träger finden?
I have three pieces of hand-luggage and two of heavy luggage	Ich habe drei Stück Handgepäck und zwei Stück großes Gepäck
Please take my luggage to a taxi	Bitte bringen Sie mein Gepäck zu einem Taxi

Sea Travel	*Die Seefahrt*
harbour	der Hafen, ⸚
sea	die See; das Meer, -e
lake	der See, -n
river	der Fluß, ⸚sse
ferry	die Fähre, -n
crossing	die Überfahrt
hovercraft	das Luftkissenboote
hovercraft terminal	die Anlegestelle für Luftkissenboot
ship	das Schiff, -e
steamer	der Dampfer, -
freighter	der Frachtdampfer, -
sailing boat	das Segelschiff, -e
rowing boat	das Ruderboot, -e

TRAVEL

motor boat	das Motorboot, -e
life-boat	das Rettungsboot, -e
life-belt	der Rettungsgürtel, -
captain	der Kapitän, -e
sailor	der Matrose, -en
steward, -ess	der Steward, die Stewardeß
cabin	die Kabine
deckchair	der Liegestuhl, ⸚e
landing ticket	die Landungskarte, -en
sea-sick	seekrank

Air Travel — *Die Luftfahrt*

aeroplane	das Flugzeug, -e
jumbo-jet	der Jumbo-jet
supersonic airliner	das Übershallflugzeug
flying	das fliegen
airport	der Flughafen
flight	der Flug
departure	Abflug
arrival	Ankunft

landing	Landung
forced landing	Notlandung
safety belt	der Sicherheitsriemen
pilot	der Pilot
air hostess	die Luftstewardeß
air-sick	luftkrank
cotton wool	die Watte
weather report	der Wetterbericht
cancelled	annulliert
postponed	verschoben
flight number ...	Flugnummer ...
departure gate	die Abflughalle
duty-free lounge	der 'Duty-free' Aufenthaltsraum
boarding ticket	die Bordkarte
delay due to	Verzögerung infolge
engine trouble	technischer Schwierigkeiten
fog	Nebel
in-flight meal	Mahlzeit an Bord
baggage allowance	Zulässiges Gepäck
charter flight	Charterflug

TRAVEL

arrival hall	die Ankunftshalle
luggage collection area	die Gepäcksammelstelle
airport 'bus	der Flughafenbus
air terminal	die Stadthaltestelle

Motoring — *der Autoverkehr*

motor car	das Auto, -s; der Wagen, -
motor bicycle	das Motorrad, ¨-er
scooter	der Roller, -
lorry	der Lastwagen, -
sports car	der Sportwagen
6-cylinder engine	der Sechszylindermotor
V8 engine	der V8-motor
coupé	das Coupé
estate car	der Kombiwagen
land-rover	der Geländewagen
petrol	das Benzin
oil	das Oel
water	das Wasser
to fill up	auffüllen

to add	zugeben
anti-freeze	das Frostschutzmittel, -
to check	prüfen
oil-level	der Oelstand
engine	der Motor
tyre pressure	der Reifendruck
to clean	reinigen
to repair	reparieren
to adjust	richten
to examine	nachsehen
to renew	auswechseln
to put in	einsetzen
to garage	unterstellen
petrol station	die Tankstelle, -n
self-service petrol station	die Selbstebedienungstankstelle
repair shop	die Reparaturwerkstätte, -n
garage	die Garage
car park	der Parkplatz, ⸚e
car park attendant	der Parkwächter, -

TRAVEL

to park	parken
to drive	fahren
driving licence	der Führerschein
insurance	die Versicherung
registration	die Registrierung
breakdown	die Panne
puncture	der Reifendefekt
to wash	waschen
to grease	schmieren
to oil	ölen
to tow in	abschleppen
the make (of a car)	die Marke
International driving permit	der internationale Führerschein
to double-de-clutch	zweimal auskuppeln
to 'rev'	aufdrehen, auf Touren bringen
motorway	die Autobahn
I need the car by ... o'clock	Ich brauche den Wagen bis ... Uhr
this morning	heute Vormittag

this afternoon	heute Nachmittag
this evening	heute Abend
tomorrow morning	morgen früh
When will the work be finished?	Wann ist die Arbeit fertig?
How much will the repair cost?	Was wird die Reparatur kosten?
What have I to pay?	Wieviel habe ich zu zahlen?

Motoring Glossary

Accelerator pedal	das Gaspedal
air compresser	der Luftpresser
air cooling system	die Luftkühlung
air filter	der Luftfilter
axle	die Achse
backfire	knallen
battery (to charge)	die Batterie (aufladen)
bonnet	die Haube
bonnet fasteners	die Haubenhalter
brakes	die Bremse, -n
brake fluid	die Bremsflüssigkeit
bulb	die Birne, -n

TRAVEL

bumper	die Stoßstange
camshaft	die Nockenwelle
carburettor	der Vergaser
chassis	das Fahrgestell
clutch	die Kuppelung
connection	der Anschluß, -sse
consumption	der Verbrauch
crankshaft	die Kurbelwelle
crankcase	das Kurbelgehäuse
cylinder	der Zylinder
Diesel engine	der Dieselmotor
differential	der Achsantrieb
direction indicator (semaphore)	der Winker
direction indicator (flashing)	der Blinker
distributor	der Verteiler
door; -handle; -lock	die Tür, -en; der Türgriff, -e; das Türschloß, -er
engine; four-stroke; two-stroke	der Motor; der Viertaktmotor; Zweitaktmotor
exhaust pipe	der Auspuff

fan	der Ventilator
fan belt	der Ventilatorriemen
foot brake	die Fußbremse, -n
filter	der Filter, -
fuel; -tank	der Kraftstoff, -e; der Kraftstoffbehälter, -
fuse	die Sicherung, -en
gasket	die Dichtung
gear; first-, second, top	die Schaltung; erster Gang; zweiter Gang; höchster Gang
gearbox	das Schaltgetriebe
generator	die Lichtmaschine
handbrake	die Handbremse
headlight	der Scheinwerfer, -
heater	die Heizung
hinge	das Scharnier, -e
horn; to hoot	das Horn, die Hupe; hupen
hydrolastic suspension	die hydropneumatische Federung
inflate	aufpumpen
ignition	die Zündung

TRAVEL

jack	der Wagenheber
jet	die Düse, -n
key	der Schlüssel, -
lighting system	die Beleuchtung
lubrication	die Schmierung
mixture; two-stroke-; fuel-air-	das Gemisch; Zweitaktgemisch; Luftgemisch
nut	die Mutter, -n
oil-filter; -pipe; -tank	der Oelfilter; die Oelleitung; der Oelbehälter
overheated	überhitzt
petrol; -tank; -can; -engine; -gauge	das Benzin; der Benzinbehälter; der Kanister; der Vergaser-motor; der Krafstoffanzeiger
pliers	die Zange
pressure gauge	das Manometer
pump	die Pumpe
radiator	der Kühler
reflector	der Reflektor
reversing light	Rückfahrscheinwerfer

to skid	schleudern
screw; -driver	die Schraube; der Schraubenzieher
sidelight	das Seitenlicht -er
spanner	der Schraubenschlüssel
spare parts; -wheel	Ersatzteile; das Ersatzrad, ⸚er
sparking plug	die Zündkerze, -n
spring	die Feder, -n
starter	der Anlasser
steering gear; -wheel	die Lenkung; das Lenkrad
tail light	das Rücklicht, -er
tappets	die Ventilschäfte
transmission	der Achsenantrieb
tyre; -lever; -valve	der Reifen; der Montierhebel; das Schlauchventil
valve	das Ventil, -e
ventilation	die Entlüftung
washer	die Scheibe, -n
wheel; front-; back-.	das Rad, ⸚er; das Vorderrad, ⸚er; das Hinterrad, ⸚er

TRAVEL

window	das Fenster, -
windscreen; -wiper	die Windschutzscheibe; der Scheibenreiniger
the ... does not work properly	der (die, das) ... ist nicht in Ordnung

Road Signs — *Verkehrszeichen*

danger	Gefahr
diversion	Umleitung
cross roads	Kreuzung
slippery	Schleudergefahr
level crossing	Eisenbahnübergang
closed to all vehicles	Verkehrsverbot
bend	Kurve
no entry	Keine Einfahrt
no stopping	Halteverbot
no parking	Parkverbot
speed limit	Höchstgeschwindigkeit
end of speed limit	Ende der Geschwindigkeitsbeschränkung

major road ahead	Vorfahrt beachten
no overtaking	Überholverbot
one way street	Einbahnstraße
major road	Hauptverkehrsstraße
entry	Einfahrt
exit	Ausfahrt
deformed surface	Unebenheiten
ice	Glatteisgefahr
frost damage	Frostschäden
steep gradient	Starkes Gefälle
bad road	Schlechte Fahrbahn
road narrows	Verengte Fahrbahn
two-way traffic	Gegenverkehr
slow	Langsam fahren
no through road	Keine Durchfahrt
keep right	Rechts fahren
turn right	Rechts abbiegen
overtake with caution	Vorsicht beim Ueberholen
fallen rock	Steinschlag

TRAVEL

oncoming traffic has right of way	Gegenverkehr hat Vorfahrt
dangerous junction	Gefährliche Einmündung
end of motorway	Ende der Autobahn
entry to premises only	Nur für Anlieger

ACCOMMODATION

to find accommodation	Unterkunft finden
for one night	für eine Nacht
for a week	für eine Woche
for a few days	für einige Tage
with full board	mit voller Verpflegung
with breakfast	mit Frühstück
with cooking facilities	mit Kochgelegenheit
in a private house	in einem Privathaus
in a hotel (inn)	in einem Hotel (Gasthaus)
in a youth hostel	in einer Jugendherberge
to hire a tent (a villa)	ein Zelt (eine Villa) mieten
to pitch a tent	ein Zelt aufschlagen
a camping site; a caravan	ein Lagerplatz; ein Wohnwagen
washing facilities	Waschgelegenheit
drinking water	Trinkwasser

ACCOMMODATION

heating	die Heizung
central heating	die Zentralheizung
gas (electric) heating	die Gas (elektrische) Heizung
coal (oil) heating	die Kohlen (Oel) Heizung
bathroom; lavatory	das Badezimmer; die Toilette
boarding house	die Pension, -en
furnished room	das möblierte Zimmer
apartment (flat)	die Wohnung
bedroom; living room	das Schlafzimmer; das Wohnzimmer
dining room; kitchen	das Speisezimmer; die Küche
landlord; landlady	der Wirt; die Wirtin
rent; receipt	die Miete; die Quittung
key; -to the flat; -to the room; -to the house	der Schlüssel; der Wohnungsschlüssel; der Zimmerschlüssel; der Hausschlüssel
to give notice	kündigen
a week's (month's) notice	wöchentliche (monatliche) Kündigung
to move in: -out; removal	einziehen; ausziehen; der Umzug

At the Hotel

Can you recommend me a hotel?	Können Sie mir ein Hotel empfehlen?
Have you any rooms vacant?	Haben Sie Zimmer frei?
a single room; a double room	ein Einzelzimmer; ein Doppelzimmer
a double bed; two single beds	ein Doppelbett; zwei Einzelbetten
a room with private bath	ein Zimmer mit Bad
bedroom and sittingroom	Schlafzimmer und Wohnzimmer
What is the price per day (week, month)?	Was kostet es pro Tag (Woche, Monat)?
I will take this room	Ich nehme dieses Zimmer
Have my luggage sent up, please	Bitte lassen Sie mein Gepäck heraufbringen
Have my luggage fetched from the station	Lassen Sie mein Gepäck vom Bahnhof holen
I should like to take a bath	Ich möchte ein Bad nehmen
The hot water tap does not work	Der Warmwasserhahn funktioniert nicht
The electric light	Das elektrische Licht

Im Hotel

ACCOMMODATION

The heating	die Heizung
Please let me have some soap	Bringen Sie mir bitte etwas Seife
a towel	ein Handtuch
another towel	noch ein Handtuch
another pillow	noch ein Kissen
another blanket	noch eine Decke
Please have this washed (cleaned)	Lassen Sie das bitte waschen (reinigen)
(pressed) ironed	plätten (bügeln)
I am leaving tomorrow morning	Ich fahre morgen früh ab
Please let me have my bill	Ich möchte die Rechnung haben
Will you get me a taxi, please	Wollen Sie mir bitte ein Taxi besorgen
Will you please take down my luggage	Wollen Sie bitte mein Gepäck herunterbringen

lounge; reception desk; lift	die Halle; das Empfangsbüro; der Fahrstuhl
receptionist; manager; cashier	der Empfangsherr; der Geschäftsführer; der Kassierer or die Kassiererin
porter; "boots"; chambermaid	der Portier; der Hausdiener; das Zimmermädchen
dining room; writing room	der Speisesaal; das Schreibzimmer
bell; service; tip	die Klingel; die Bedienung; das Trinkgeld

TAKING A FURNISHED ROOM

May I see the landlady?	Kann ich die Wirtin sprechen?
Have you a room to let?	Haben Sie ein Zimmer zu ver-...mieten?
The ... Agency has given me your address	Ich habe Ihre Adresse von der ... Agentur
I saw your advertisement in the newspaper	Ich sah Ihre Anzeige in der Zeitung
May I see the room?	Kann ich das Zimmer sehen?
Haven't you a larger (smaller) room	Haben Sie kein grösseres (kleineres) Zimmer
Do you provide full board?	Geben Sie volle Pension?
Just bed and breakfast	Nur Zimmer und Frühstück
What is the price per week (month)?	Wie ist die Miete pro Woche (Monat)?

I shall be staying about . . . weeks (months)	Ich bleibe etwa . . . Wochen (Monate)
Does this include electricity?	Ist Elektrizität eingeschlossen?
May I also see the other room?	Kann ich auch das andere Zimmer sehen?
This will suit me alright, I'll take it	Dies gefällt mir. Ich nehme es
I shall leave you a deposit	Ich werde Ihnen eine Anzahlung lassen
May I move in in the afternoon?	Kann ich am Nachmittag einziehen?
Payment in advance (weekly notice) is usual, isn't it?	Vorauszahlung (wöchentliche Kündigung) ist üblich, nicht wahr?

ASKING THE WAY

Where is the road to . . . ?	Wo ist die Straße nach . . . ?
Where does this road go to?	Wohin führt diese Straße?
In what direction is . . . ?	In welcher Richtung liegt . . . ?
Does this road lead to . . . ?	Führt diese Straße nach . . . ?
Excuse me, where is the bus stop?	Entschuldigen Sie, wo ist die Autobushaltestelle?
Where can I find a bus to . . . ?	Wo kann ich einen Autobus nach . . . bekommen?
Does this bus go to . . . ?	Fährt dieser Autobus nach . . . ?
In what direction must I go?	In welche Richtung muß ich fahren?
Where do I have to get off?	Wo muß ich aussteigen?
Do I get out here?	Muß ich hier aussteigen?
Which way do I go to . . . ?	Wie komme ich von hier nach . . . ?

Would you be good enough to direct me to ...?	Können Sie mir bitte sagen wie ich nach ... komme?
Is it far from here to ...?	Ist es von hier weit nach ...?
Can I walk there?	Kann ich zu Fuß gehen?
Go straight on	Gehen Sie geradeaus
Take the first on the right	Nehmen Sie die erste Strßae rechts
The second to the left	Die zweite links
Near here	Hier in der Nähe
Far from here	Weit von hier
On the right	Rechts
On the left	Links
To the right	Nach rechts
To the left	Nach links
At the corner	An der Ecke
Tramway (Streetcar)	Die Strassenbahn
Underground (Subway)	Die Untergrundbahn
The nearest underground station. (Petrol station, bus stop)	Die nächste Untergrundbahnstation. (Tankstelle, Autobushaltestelle)

ASKING THE WAY

Taxi	Das Taxi
A main road	Eine Hauptstraße
A side road	Eine Seitenstraße
Cross roads	Die Straßenkreuzung
To cross the road	Die Straße überqueren
A fork (in the road)	Eine Abzweigung

SHOPS AND SHOPPING

shop (small)	Der Laden
business-house (wholesale or retail)	Das Geschäft
department stores	Das Kaufhaus
supermarket	der Supermarket
cash-and-wrap	Kasse
to buy	kaufen
to sell	verkaufen
sold	verkauft
to pay	bezahlen
paid	bezahlt
I'd like some soap	Ich möchte etwas Seife
Have you got any razor blades?	Haben Sie Rasierklingen?
How many do you want?	Wieviele möchten Sie haben?
A dozen. A few	Ein Dutzend. Ein paar

SHOPS AND SHOPPING

A pound. Half a pound	Ein Pfund. Ein halbes Pfund
How much is that?	Was kostet das?
How much are these?	Was kosten diese?
Will you show me some stationery?	Bitte zeigen Sie mir etwas Briefpapier?
I want something like this	Ich möchte etwas in dieser Art
What is the price of that dressing-gown in the window?	Was kostet der Schlafrock, den Sie im Fenster haben?
I should like to see some of the fountain-pens you have advertised	Ich möchte mir mal einige von den Füllfederhaltern ansehen, die Sie annonciert haben
How much did you say this one was?	Was sagten Sie doch, kostet dieser?
No, that is not quite what I want	Das ist nicht ganz, was ich suche
I don't like these	Diese gefallen mir nicht
I don't quite care for this style	Dieser Stil sagt mir nicht zu
Can you show me something different?	Können Sie mir etwas anderes zeigen?
That is not the right size (colour)	Das ist nicht die richtige Grösse (Farbe)

Haven't you anything	bigger smaller thicker thinner darker lighter better cheaper stronger more like this?	Haben Sie nichts	größeres? kleineres? dickeres? dünneres? dunkleres? helleres? besseres? billigeres? stärkeres? mehr in dieser Art?

Like that one you showed me just now, but slightly larger — Wie das, was Sie mir vorhin zeigten, nur etwas größer

How much a yard is it? — Was kostet der Meter?

That is more than I intended paying — Das ist mehr als ich ausgeben wollte

I'll take this pair — Ich nehme dieses Paar

I'll take these two — Ich nehme diese beiden

How much is that altogether, please? — Was macht das zusammen, bitte?

That's all, thank you — Danke das ist alles

Here's a one-pound note — Hier ist ein Pfundschein

SHOPS AND SHOPPING

| Good afternoon, I'm much obliged to you | Guten Tag und schönen Dank auch |

Colours / *Farben*

black	schwarz
blue	blau
brown	braun
dark	dunkel
green	grün
grey	grau
light	hell
pink	rosa
red	rot
white	weiß
yellow	gelb

Something in { silk / wool / cotton / linen / leather }

etwas in { Seide / Wolle / Baumwolle / Leinen / Leder }

metal	Metall
gold	Gold
silver	Silber
wood	Holz
glass	Glas

Baker — *der Bäcker*

baker's shop	die Bäckerei
bread	das Brot
loaf	ein Brot
a roll	ein Brötchen
cake	der Kuchen
buns	das Gebäck
croissant	das Hörnchen

Bank — *die Bank*

Do you use the eurocheque system? — Verwenden Sie das Euroscheck-System?

Can you cash these travellers' cheques? — Kann ich bei Ihnen diese Reiseschecks eintauschen?

Do you take credit cards? — Akzeptieren Sie Kreditkarten?

SHOPS AND SHOPPING

Bookseller	*der Buchhändler*
bookshop	die Buchhandlung
dictionary	das Wörterbuch
phrase book	der Sprachführer
guide book	der Reiseführer
map	die Landkarte
English novel	der englische Roman
English romance	der englische Liebesroman
Bootmaker	*der Schuhmacher*
a pair of shoes (boots)	ein Paar Schuhe (Stiefel)
made to measure	nach Maß machen
to mend	reparieren
to sole	besohlen
to heel	Absätze machen
shoe-lace	das Schuhband
shoe-polish	das Schuhputzmittel
Butcher	*der Fleischer*
butcher's shop	die Fleischerei

meat	das Fleisch
sausages	die Würstchen
(dry) sausage	die Wurst
Chemist's	*die Drogerie*
dispensary	die Apotheke
soap	die Seife
razor	das Rasiermesser
safety razor	der Rasierapparat
razor blade	die Rasierklinge
shaving-soap	die Rasierseife
shaving-brush	der Rasierpinsel
lipstick	der Lippenstift
powder	der Puder
scent	das Parfum
cream	die Creme
tooth-brush	die Zahnbürste
tooth-paste	die Zahnpaste
aspirin	Aspirin
vaseline	die Vaseline

SHOPS AND SHOPPING

iodine	Jod
cotton-wool	die Watte
bicarbonate of soda	doppel-kohlensaures Natron
castor oil	Rizinusöl
cordial drops	Magentropfen
sleeping draught	ein Schlafmittel
deodorant	das Deodorant

Clothing *Kleidung*
(see also *Laundry, Hosier, Tailor*)

dress	das Kleid, -er
blouse	die Bluse, -n
skirt	der Rock, ⸚e
jacket	die Jacke, -n
costume	das Kostüm, -e
suit	der Anzug, ⸚e
trousers	die Hose, -n
waistcoat	die Weste, -n
material	der Stoff, -e

overcoat	der Mantel, ⸚
cardigan	die Strickjacke
mini-skirt	der Minirock
midi-skirt	der Midirock
maxi-coat	der Maximantel
dinner jacket	der Smoking

Dairy — *das Milchgeschäft*

milk	die Milch
butter	die Butter
eggs	die Eier
cheese	der Käse

Electrical shop — *das Elektrogeschäft*

This is broken	das ist kaputt
Can you mend it?	Können Sie es reparieren
radio	das Radio
television	das Fernsehen
fan	der Ventilator
heater	der Heizofen

SHOPS AND SHOPPING 133

washing machine	die Waschmaschine
spin drier	die Schleudermaschine
vacuum cleaner	der Staubsauger
mixer	der Mixer
blender	die Küchenmaschine
light	das Licht
oven	der Ofen
stove	der Herd
grill	der Grill
bell	die Klingel
hotplate	die Warmhalteplatte
switch	der Schalter
time-switch	der Zeitschalter
electric blanket	die Heizdecke
refrigerator	der Kühlschrank
electric carving knife	das Tranchiermesser
fuse	die Sicherung
fuse-wire	der Sicherungsdraht
electric generator	der elektrische Generator
light bulb	die Glühbirne

socket	die Steckdose
5-amp plug	der 5-Ampère-Stecker
adaptor	der Zwischenstecker
Fishmonger's	*das Fischgeschäft*
fish	der Fisch
Market	*der Markt*
stall	der Stand, ⸚e
Newsvendor	*der Zeitungsverkäufer*
newspaper kiosk	der Zeitungskiosk
newspaper	die Zeitung, -en
morning paper	die Morgenzeitung
evening paper	die Abendzeitung
magazine	die Zeitschrift, -en
Optician	*der Optiker*
spectacles	die Brille
frame	der Rahmen

SHOPS AND SHOPPING

Pastry shop	*die Konditorei*
(fancy) cake	die Torte, -n
(assorted) pastries	das Törtchen, -
ice cream	das Eis
Camera Shop	*das Fotogeschäft*
black and white film	der Schwarzweißfilm
colour film	der Farbfilm
cartridge film	der Kassettenfilm
for slides	für Diapositive
for prints	für Abzüge
fast film	der hochempfindliche Film
slow film	ein Film mit niedriger Empfindlichkeit
can you develop this?	Können Sie diesen Film entwickeln
can you load (unload) this camera?	Können Sie diesen Film einlegen (ausspannen)
flashgun	das Blitzgerät
flashbulbs	die Blitzbirnen
aperture	die Blende

lens	das Objektiv
shutter speed adjustment	die Einstellung der Verschluß geschwindigkeit
negative	das Negativ
can you print this?	können Sie hiervon Abzüge machen?
can you enlarge this?	können Sie hiervon Vergrößerungen machen?
contact prints	die Kontaktabzüge
polaroid film	der Polaroid-Film

Stationer's — *das Papierwarengeschäft*

pencil	der Bleistift, -e
biro	der Kugelschreiber, -
fountain pen	der Füllfederhalter, -
nib; penholder	die Feder, n; der Federhalter, -
ink; blotting paper	die Tinte; das Löschpapier
note-paper; envelope	das Briefpapier; der Umschlag, ⸚e
packing paper; toilet paper	das Packpapier; das Toilettenpapier
paper handkerchiefs	Papiertaschentücher

SHOPS AND SHOPPING

Sweet shop	*das Konfitürengeschäft*
sweet; candy	**der Bonbon, -s**
chocolate	**die Schokolade, -n**
a box of chocolates	**ein Kasten Konfekt**
Department store	*das Warenhaus; das Kaufhaus*
department	**die Abteilung, -en**
cash desk	**die Kasse**
Fruit Shop	*das Obstgeschäft*
Greengrocer's	*das Obst und Gemüsegeschäft*
Grocer's	*das Lebensmittelgeschäft*

see food list on p. 77

Haberdashery	*Kurzwaren*
thread	**der Zwirn**
needle(s)	**die Nadel(n)**
pin(s)	**die Stecknadel(n)**

safety pin(s)	Die Sicherheitsnadel(n)
button(s)	der Knopf, die Knöpfe
zip fastener	der Reißverschluß

Hairdresser	*der Frisör*
shave, please	bitte rasieren
haircut	Haarschneiden
not too short	nicht zu kurz
rather short	ziemlich kurz
water wave	die Wasserwelle
iron wave	die Ondulation
permanent wave	die Dauerwelle
shampoo	Kopfwaschen
trim	ein Haarschnitt
a re-style	eine neue Frisur
shampoo and set	Waschen und Legen

Hosier	*das Strumpfgeschäft*
stockings	die Strümpfe
socks	die Socken

(See also *laundry*)

SHOPS AND SHOPPING

Jeweller	*der Juwelier*
jewel(s)	die Juwele(n)
ring	der Ring, -e
bracelet	das Armband, ̈-er
brooch	die Brosche, -n
necklace	die Halskette, -n
Laundry	*die Wäscherei*
linen	die Wäsche
laundry list	die Wäscheliste
shirt	das Hemd -en
collar	der Kragen, -
vest	das Unterhemd, -en
pants, slip	die Unterhose, -n
towel	das Handtuch, ̈-er
handkerchief	das Taschentuch, ̈-er
combinations	die Hemdhose, -n
knickers	der Schlüpfer, -
night shirt or nightdress	das Nachthemd, -en
pyjamas	die Pyjamas

Tailor	*der Schneider*
man's suit	der Anzug, ⸚e
lady's costume (suit)	das Kostüm, -e
Tobacconist	*Der Zigarettenladen*
cigarette	die Zigarette, -n
cigar	die Zigarre, -n
pipe	die Pfeife, -n
tobacco	der Tabak
lighter	das Feuerzeug, -e
match	das Streichholz, ⸚er
a box of matches	eine Schachtel Streichhölzer
roll-your-own cigarettes tobacco	Rollen Sie Ihre Zigaretten selbst Ihren Tabak selbst
Watchmaker	*Der Uhrmacher*
wrist watch	die Armbanduhr, -en
alarm clock	der Wecker
to repair	reparieren
watch-strap	das Uhrarmband, ⸚er

THE POST OFFICE AND TELEPHONE

The Post-office	*Das Postamt*
Where is the nearest post-office?	Wo ist das nächste Postamt?
What is the postage, please?	Wie hoch ist das Porto?
I want to register this letter	Ich möchte diesen Brief einschreiben lassen
Are there any letters for me?	Sind Briefe für mich da?
Please forward my mail to this address	Bitte senden Sie meine Briefe an diese Adresse
stamp	die Briefmarke, -n
postcard	die Postkarte, -n
air-mail	die Luftpost
letter-box	der Briefkasten, ⸚
telegram	das Telegramm, -e
money-order	dis Postanweisung, -en
parcel	das Paket, -e

registered letter	der eingeschriebene Brief
to have registered	einschreiben lassen
telephone	das Telefon
	der Fernsprecher
to phone	telefonieren
to ring up	anrufen
telephone number	die Telefonnummer
telephone directory	das Telefonbuch
phone-box	die Telefonzelle
I wish to phone to London	Ich möchte mit London sprechen

EATING AND DRINKING

What will you have, tea or coffee?	Was nehmen Sie, Tee oder Kaffee?
Do you take sugar and milk in your tea?	Nehmen Sie Milch und Zucker in Ihren Tee?
Only milk, no sugar, thank you	Nur Milch, keinen Zucker, bitte
Will you have some Toast with your tea?	Möchten Sie Toast zu Ihrem Tee?
Thank you I will take some	Danke, gern
Would you be so kind as to pass me the salt?	Würden Sie so gut sein, mir das Salz herüberzureichen?
Can I pass you anything?	Kann ich Ihnen etwas reichen?
May I help you to some more meat?	Darf ich Ihnen noch etwas Fleisch geben?
Just a little please	Nur ein wenig, bitte
No thank you	Nein, danke

No, I won't have any more, thank you	Nein, ich möchte wirklich nicht mehr, danke schön
No; I enjoyed it very much, but I won't have any more	Nein, danke. Es hat mir wirklich sehr gut geschmeckt. Aber ich will wirklich nichts mehr
Will you have a glass of wine?	Trinken Sie ein Glas Wein?
May I pour you out another glass?	Darf ich Ihnen noch ein Glas eingießen?
May I peel an orange for you?	Kann ich Ihnen eine Orange schälen?
Have some more pudding?	Nehmen Sie noch etwas Pudding?
Won't you help yourself to some ...	Nehmen Sie sich doch etwas ...
Are you fond of ...	Essen Sie gern ...
It's my favourite dish	Es ist meine Lieblingsspeise
Not very much, if you will forgive my frankness	Offen gestanden, nicht besonders
How did you like the ...?	Wie hat Ihnen ... geschmeckt?
It was excellent (delicious)	Ausgezeichnet (Ganz hervorragend)

EATING AND DRINKING

Restaurant	*Das Restaurant*
waiter	der Kellner
A table for two	Ein Tisch für zwei
The menu	Die Speisekarte
The wine-list	Die Weinliste
The set meal	Das Menü
Can you recommend this?	Können Sie das empfehlen?
A knife (fork, spoon) is missing	Ein Messer (eine Gabel, ein Löffel) fehlt
Waiter, the bill please	Ober, die Rechnung bitte
You can keep the change	Es ist in Ordnung
fork	Die Gabel, -n
knife	Das Messer, -
spoon	Der Löffel, -
plate	Der Teller, -
dish	Die Schüssel, -n
breakfast	Das Frühstück
to have breakfast	frühstücken
lunch	Das Mittagessen
to dine	Zu Mittag essen

supper	Das Abendbrot
to have supper	Abendbrot essen
boiled	gekocht
braised; stewed	geschmort
baked	gebacken
fried; roasted	gebraten
minced	gehackt
grilled	geröstet
salted	gesalzen
well done	gut durchgebraten
underdone	leicht durchgebraten
it is good	es ist gut
bad	schlecht
hot	scharf
sweet	süß
burnt	angebrannt
hot	heiß
cold	kalt
raw	roh

EATING AND DRINKING

Food	*Speisen*
apple	der Apfel, ⸚
apricot	die Aprikose, -n
asparagus	der Spargel
bacon	der Speck
banana	die Banane, -n
beans	die Bohnen
french beans	grüne Bohnen
beef	das Rindfleisch
beef steak	das Beefsteak
beetroot	rote Rübe, -n
biscuit	der Keks; das Biskuit, -s
bread	das Brot
slice of bread and butter	das Butterbrot, -e
breast	die Brust
butter	die Butter
brussel sprouts	der Rosenkohl
cabbage	der Kohl
carrot	die Karotte, -n
cauliflower	der Blumenkohl

celery	der Sellerie
cherry	die Kirsche, -n
chocolate	Schokolade
chop	das Kotelett, -s
cream	die Sahne
cucumber	die Gurke, -n
date	die Dattel, -n
dessert	die Nachspeise
duck	die Ente
eel	der Aal, -e
egg	das, Ei,-er
boiled egg	das gekochte Ei
fried egg	das Spiegelei
hard boiled	hart gekocht
soft boiled	weich gekocht
scrambled egg	das Rührei
fig	die Feige, -n
fish	der Fisch, -e
fruit	das Obst
stewed fruit	der Kompott

EATING AND DRINKING

grapes	die Weintrauben
game	das Wild
goose	die Gans, ⸚e
gravy	die Sauce, -n
ham	der Schinken
raw	roh
cooked	gekocht
hare	der Hase, -n
herring	der Hering, -e
honey	der Honig
hors d'oeuvre	die Vorspeise
jam	die Konfitüre, -n
ice-cream	das Eis
jelly	der Gelee
kidney	die Niere
lamb	das Lamm
lemon	die Zitrone, -n
lentil	die Linse, -n
lettuce	der Kopfsalat
liver	die Leber

lobster	der Hummer
meat	das Fleisch
melon	die Melone
macaroni	die Macaroni
marmalade	die Marmelade
mayonnaise	die Mayonnaise
mushrooms	der Pilz, -e
mustard	der Mostrich (Senf)
mutton	das Hammelfleisch
oil	das Oel
olive	die Olive
nut	die Nuß, ⸚sse
omelet	das Omelett
onion	die Zwiebel, -n
orange	die Apfelsine, -n
oyster	die Auster, -n
pancake	der Eierkuchen
peach	der Pfirsich, -e
pea	die Erbse, -n
pear	die Birne, -n

EATING AND DRINKING

pepper	der Pfeffer
pie	die Pastete, -n
pineapple	die Ananas
plum	die Pflaume, -n
pork	das Schweinefleisch
potato	die Kartoffel, -n
fried potatoes	Bratkartoffeln
boiled potatoes	Salzkartoffeln
mashed potatoes	Kartoffelbrei
poultry	das Geflügel, -
wing	der Flügel, -
leg	die Keule, -n
prawn	die Garnele, -n
prune	die Backpflaume, -n
rabbit	das Kaninchen, -
raspberry	die Himbeere, -n
rhubarb	der Rhabarber
rice	der Reis
roast beef	der Rinderbraten
roast pork	der Schweinebraten

roast veal	der Kalbsbraten
roll	das Brötchen, -
rusk	der Zwiebäck, -e
salad	der Salat, -e
salmon	der Lachs
salt	das Salz
sandwich	das belegte Brot
cheese sandwich	Käsebrot
ham sandwich	Schinkenbrot
sausage sandwich	Wurstbrot
sausage	die Wurst, ⸚e
hot dogs	die Würstchen
shrimp	die Krabbe, -n
snack	der Imbiß
soup	die Suppe, -n
sole	die Seezunge, -n
spinach	der Spinat
spaghetti	die Spagetti
sardine	die Sardine, -n
sauce	die Sauce, -n

EATING AND DRINKING

steak	das Beefsteak, -s
strawberry	die Erdbeere, -n
sugar	der Zucker
tomato	die Tomate, -n
tongue	die Zunge, -n
trout	die Forelle, -n
turkey	die Pute, -n
veal	das Kalbfleisch
vegetable	das Gemüse, -
vinegar	der Essig

Drinks	*Getränke*
tankard	das Seidel, -; der Krug, ⁼e
glass	ein Glas, ⁼er
cup	eine Tasse, -n
bottle	eine Flasche, -n
carafe	eine Karaffe, -n
a pot	ein Kännchen

Non-Alcoholic	*Alkoholfrei*
coffee	der Kaffee
black coffee	schwarzer Kaffee
with milk	mit Milch
iced	Eiskaffee
tea	der Tee
with lemon	mit Zitrone
beef-tea	die Fleischbrühe
chocolate	die Schokolade
cocoa	der Kakao
milk	Milch
water	das Wasser
mineral water	das Mineralwasser, -
lemonade	die Zitronenlimonade, -n
lemon squash	Zitrone naturell
orangeade	die Orangeade, -n
orange juice	der Orangensaft
soda water	das Sodawasser

EATING AND DRINKING

Alcoholic	**Alkoholisch**
beer	**das Bier, -e**
a small glass of light beer	**ein kleines helles**
a large glass of dark beer	**ein grosses dunkles**
lager	**das Lagerbier**
wine	**der Wein, -e**
white wine	**der Weißwein**
red wine	**der Rotwein**
local wine	**der hiesige** (in Austria:) **der heurige**
hock	**der Rheinwein**
burgundy	**der Burgunderwein**
sweet wine	**der Süßwein**
port	**der Portwein**
dry	**herb**
vermouth	**der Wermut**
claret	**der Bordeauxwein**
cider	**der Apfelwein**
champagne	**der Sekt**
brandy	**der Branntwein, -e**

liqueur	der Likör, -e
cordial	der Magenlikör, -e
rum	der Rum

MONEY

Money	*Das Geld*
I wish to change English money into German	Ich möchte englisches Geld in deutsches umwechseln
to cash travellers' cheques	Reiseschecks einlösen
banknote	der Geldschein, -e
small change	Kleingeld
a ten mark note	ein Zehnmarkschein
a fifty Pfennig piece	ein Pfünfzigpfennigstück, -e
pound sterling	das englische Pfund, -e
American Dollar	der amerikanische Dollar, -s
bank	die Bank, -en
cheque	der Scheck, -s
receipt	die Quittung, -en
rate of exchange	der Kurs, -e

German coin and banknotes are as below:

1 Deutsche Mark (DM) = 100 Pfennige (pfg.

Münzen (coins):
- 1 pfg.
- 2 pfg.
- 5 pfg.
- 10 pfg.
- 50 pfg.
- 1 DM
- 2 DM
- 5 DM

Banknoten (bank notes):
- 5 DM
- 10 DM
- 50 DM
- 100 DM
- 500 DM
- 1.000 DM

THE WEATHER AND THERMOMETER

The Weather
What is the weather like to-day?
it is cold (cool)
it is hot (warm)
I am cold (warm)
it is fine
it is raining
it is snowing
it is windy
it is stormy
it is foggy
it is freezing
the sky is clear (cloudy)
the sun shines

Das Wetter
Wie ist das Wetter heute?
Es ist kalt (kühl)
es ist heiß (warm)
mir ist kalt (warm)
es ist schön
es regnet
es schneit
es ist windig
es ist stürmisch
es ist neblig
es friert
der Himmel ist klar (bewölkt)
die Sonne scheint

Thermometer
Fahrenheit

Das Thermometer
Celsius

Fahrenheit	Celsius
−4	−20
0	−17·8
5	−15
23	5
32 freezing point	0 Gefrierpunkt (Null)
41	5
55	12·7
60	15·5
65	18·3
70	21·1
77	25
80	26·6
85	29·4
90	32·2
95	35
100	37·7
113	45
176	80
212 boiling point	100 Siedepunkt

THE WEATHER AND THERMOMETER

Note.—On the Continent the Celsius (=Centigrade) scale is employed. To turn Fahrenheit into Celsius, subtract 32 and multiply by $\frac{5}{9}$; *e.g.*

$$95°F. = (95 - 32) \times \tfrac{5}{9} = 35°C.$$

To turn Celsius into Fahrenheit, multiply by $\frac{9}{5}$ and add 32; *e.g.*

$$-5°C. = (-5 \times \tfrac{9}{5}) + 32 = 23°F.$$

TOWN AND COUNTRY

town	die Stadt, ⸚e
street	die Straße, -n
square	der Platz, ⸚e
sidewalk	der Bürgersteig, -e
roadway	der Fahrdamm
market	der Markt, ⸚e
suburb	der Vorort, -e
bridge	die Brücke, -n
river	der Fluß, ⸚sse
church	die Kirche, -n
garden	der Garten, ⸚n
park	der Park, -s
factory	die Fabrik, -en
office	das Büro, -s

TOWN AND COUNTRY

museum	das Museum
school	die Schule, -n
town-hall	das Rathaus
castle	das Schloß, ̈sser
cathedral	der Dom, -e
policeman	der Polizist, -en
police-station	die Polizei
bank	die Bank, -en
cinema	das Kino, -s
theatre	das Theater, -
hotel	das Hotel, -s
gate	das Tor, -e
letter-box	der Briefkasten, ̈
consulate	das Konsulat, -e
embassy	die Botschaft, -en

Country — *Das Land*
in the country — auf dem Lande
to the country — aufs Land
mountain — der Berg, -e

mountains, range of	das Gebirge
in the	im Gebirge
to the	ins Gebirge
valley	das Tal, ⸚er
guest-house	das Gasthaus, ⸚er
farm (small)	der Hof, ⸚e
farm (large)	das Gut, ⸚er
forest	der Wald, ⸚er
mill	die Mühle, -n
field	das Feld, -er
tree	der Baum, ⸚e
flower	die Blume, -n
meadow	die Wiese, -n
barn	die Scheune, -n
farmhouse	das Bauernhaus, ⸚er
highway	die Landstrasse, -n
hill	der Hügel, -
lake	der See, -n
pond	der Teich, -e
stream	der Bach, ⸚e

TOWN AND COUNTRY

village	das Dorf, ¨-er
spa	der Kurort, -e
place, hamlet	der Ort, -e

AT THE SEASIDE

the sea, the beach	die See; der Strand
the coast; the harbour	die Küste; der Hafen
the wave; the current(s)	die Welle; die Strömung, -en
high tide; low tide	die Flut; die Ebbe
bathing; swimming	baden; schwimmen
the sea is rough (calm)	die See ist stürmisch (ruhig)
the beach is sandy (pebbly)	der Strand ist sandig (steinig)
bathing costume; -cap	der Badeanzug, ¨e; die Badekappe, -n
bathing towel; -wrap	das Badehandtuch, ¨er; der Bademantel, ¨
beach shoes; -tent	die Strandschuhe; das Badezelt
bathing hut; pier	die Badekabine, -n; der Seesteg
life boat; -belt	das Rettungsboot, -e; der Rettungsring, -e

AT THE SEASIDE

sailing boat; rowing-	das Segelboot, -e; das Ruderboot, -e
to sail; to row	segeln; rudern
canoe; surf board	das Kanu; das Wellenbrett
surf riding; water ski-ing	Wellenreiten; Wasserski
diving; -outfit	Tauchen; Taucherausrüstung
underwater swimming	Unterwasserschwimmen
beach-ball	Strandball

THE FAMILY

The Family	*Die Familie*
Christian name	der Vorname, -n
surname	der Familienname
maiden name	der Mädchenname
parents	die Eltern
children	die Kinder
father	der Vater
mother	die Mutter
brother	der Bruder, ⸚
sister	die Schwester, -n
son	der Sohn, ⸚e
daughter	die Tochter
father-in-law	der Schwiegervater
mother-in-law	die Schweigermutter
son-in-law	der Schwiegersohn

THE FAMILY

daughter-in-law	die Schwiegertochter
brother-in-law	der Schwager
sister-in-law	die Schwägerin
half-brother	der Halbbruder
half-sister	die Halbschwester
grandfather	der Grossvater, ¨
grandmother	die Grossmutter, ¨
grandparents	die Grosseltern
grandson	der Enkel, -
granddaughter	die Enkelin, -nen
uncle	der Onkel, -
aunt	die Tante, -n
cousin (male)	der Cousin; der Vetter, -
cousin (female)	die Cousine, -n
nephew	der Neffe, -n
niece	die Nichte, -n
godfather	der Pate, -n
godmother	die Patin, -nen
born	geboren
birth	die Geburt

birthday	der Geburtstag
baptism, baptised	die Taufe; getauft
confirmation	die Einsegnung
engagement; engaged	die Verlobung; verlobt
marriage; married	die Heirat; verheiratet
the marriage ceremony	die Hochzeit
husband; wife	der Gatte; die Gattin

THE HUMAN BODY

The Human Body	*Der menschliche Körper*
hair; head	das Haar, -e; der Kopf, ⸚e
face; forehead	das Gesicht; die Stirn
ear; eye	das Ohr, -en; das Auge, -n
eyebrow; eyelash	die Augenbraue, -n; die Augenwimper, -n
nose; mouth	die Nase; der Mund
lip; tongue	die Lippe, -n; die Zunge
cheek; skin	die Wange, -n; die Haut
beard; moustache	der Bart; der Schnurrbart
neck; shoulder	der Hals; die Schulter, -n
chest; heart	die Brust, ⸚e; das Herz
lungs; stomach	die Lunge, -n; der Magen
arm; hand	der Arm, -e; die Hand, ⸚e

finger; thumb	der Finger, der Daumen,
back; spine	der Rücken; das Rückgrat
leg; knee	das Bein, -e; das Knie, -e
foot; toe	Der Fuß, ¨sse; die Zehe, -n
lame; crippled	lahm; verkrüppelt
deaf; dumb	taub; stumm
bald; blind	kahl; blind
slim; stout	schlank; dick
tall; short	groß; klein
good looking; ugly	gut aussehend; häßlich
healthy; ill	gesund; krank
health; illness	die Gesundheit; die Krankheit, -en
old; young	alt; jung
... years old	... Jahre alt
How old are you?	Wie alt sind Sie?
God bless you! Your health!	Gesundheit!

THE HUMAN BODY

Health   *die Gesundheit*

How are you?	Wie geht es Ihnen?
How is your father (your mother)?	Wie geht es Ihrem Vater (Ihrer Mutter)?
How are the children?	Wie geht es den Kindern?
Very well, thank you. And you?	Danke, sehr gut. Und Ihnen?
Fine – quite well – fairly well	Ausgezeichnet—ganz gut—einigermaßen
I am afraid not too well	Leider nicht sehr gut
What is the matter with you (him, her)?	Was fehlt Ihnen (ihm, ihr)?
You look (don't look) well	Sie sehen (nicht) gut aus
Don't you feel well?	Fühlen Sie sich nicht wohl?
I don't feel well	Ich fühle mich nicht wohl
I am ill	Ich bin krank
I have had an accident	Ich habe einen Unfall gehabt
I have caught a cold	Ich habe mich erkältet

I have ⎧ a headache   Ich habe ⎧ Kopfschmerzen
He has ⎨ a sore throat   Er hat ⎨ Halsschmerzen
She has ⎩ a temperature   Sie hat ⎩ Fieber

I have a rash	Ich habe einen Ausschlag
I have food poisoning	Ich habe eine Lebensmittelvergiftung
He has a pain in the back	Er hat Schmerzen im Rücken
She has a pain in the chest	Sie hat Schmerzen in der Brust
a pain in the stomach	Schmerzen im Magen
He broke his arm (leg)	Er hat sich den Arm (das Bein) gebrochen
She has fainted	Sie ist ohnmächtig
I feel sick	Mir ist übel
I sprained my ankle	Ich habe mir den Fuß verrenkt
I hurt my leg	Ich habe mir das Bein verletzt
There is something in my eye	Mir ist etwas ins Auge gekommen
She has had sunstroke	Sie hat einen Sonnenstich
I have a pain here	Ich habe Schmerzen hier
acute toothache	starke Zahnschmerzen
broken a tooth	einen Zahn abgebrochen
broken my plate	mein Gebiß zerbrochen

THE HUMAN BODY

Can you	relieve the pain?	Können Sie mir	den Schmerz stillen?
	fill (pull) the tooth?		den Zahn plombieren (ziehen)?
	repair the plate?		das Gebiß reparieren?

Can I have an injection? — Kann ich eine Betäubung haben?
That hurts — Das tut weh
I am allergic to penicillin — Ich bin gegen Penicillin allergisch

SPORT, AMUSEMENTS, PASTIMES

Sport	der Sport
to play	spielen
a game of . . . : a match	eine Partie . . .
sports ground	der Sportplatz
racing track	die Rennbahn
to win; won	gewinnen; gewonnen
to lose; lost	verlieren; verloren
to beat; beaten	besiegen; besiegt
player (male and female)	der Spieler, -; die Spielerin, -nen
spectator	der Zuschauer, -
the equipment	die Ausrüstung, -
to join in a game	mitspielen
to have a game	eine Partie machen

SPORT, AMUSEMENTS, PASTIMES

Archery	*Bogenschiessen*
bow	der Bogen, -
arrow	der Pfeil, -e
Athletics	*Freiübungen*
Boxing	*Boxen*
Cycling	*Radfahren*
bicycle	das Fahrrad
tyre	der Reifen
puncture	der Reifenschaden
Fencing	*Fechten*
Fishing	*Angeln*
-line	die Angelschnur
-rod	die Angelrute
-net	das Fischnetz
-boat	das Fischerboot
bait	der Köder

Football	*Fussball*
football ground	der Fussballplatz
team	die Mannschaft, -en
goal	das Tor, -e
Golf	*Golf*
-course	der Golfplatz
-club	der Golfschläger
a round	eine Runde
Mountaineering	*Bergsteigen*
to climb the ...	den ... besteigen
a guide	ein Bergführer
rope	das Seil
to rope	anseilen
axe	die Axt, ⸚e
mountain hut	die Berghütte
mountain railway	die Bergbahn
mountain top	die Bergspitze

SPORT, AMUSEMENTS, PASTIMES

Racing	*Rennen*
horse-	Pferderennen
car-	Autorennen
bicycle-	Radrennen
motor bicycle-	Motorradrennen
race course	die Rennbahn

Riding	*Reiten*
horse	das Pferd
riding stables	die Reitschule
saddle	der Sattel
riding track	die Reitbahn
riding boots	die Reitstiefel

Rowing	*Rudern*
rowing boat	das Ruderboot
oar	das Ruder

| *Shooting* | *Schiessen* |
| gun | die Flinte |

Sailing — *Segeln*
sailing boat — das Segelboot
sail — das Segel

Skating — *Schlittschuhlaufen*
skating rink — die Eisbahn
skates — die Schlittschuhe
skating boots — die Schlittschuhstiefel
roller skates — die Rollschuhe
roller skating — Rollschuhlaufen

Ski-ing — *Skilaufen*
skis — Skier
ski boots — Skistiefel
ski stick — Skistock, ¨e
ski-ing lessons — Skiunterricht
spring-board — die Sprungschanze
slope — der Abhang
snow — der Schnee
goggles — die Schutzbrille

SPORT, AMUSEMENTS, PASTIMES

Swimming
swimming bath
bathing costume
bathing cap
bathing wrap
bathing towel
bathing cabin
bathing trunks

Tennis
tennis-court
tennis ball
racket
net
table tennis
forty-fifteen
smash

Water Sports
Surf riding

Schwimmen
das Schwimmbad
der Badeanzug, ¨e
die Badekappe, -n
der Bademantel, ¨
das Badetuch, ¨er
die Badekabine, -n
die Badehose, -n

Tennis
der Tennisplatz, ¨e
der Tennisball, ¨e
der Tennisschläger, -
das Netz
Tischtennis
Vierzig-fünfzehn
der Schmetterball

Wassersport
Wellenreiten

surf board	das Wellenbrett
pedal boat	das Wasserrad
waterski	Wasserski
diving	tauchen
underwater swimming	Unterwasserschwimmen

Entertainments — *Vergnügungen*

theatre; cinema	das Theater; das Kino
opera; musical comedy	die Oper; die Operette
music hall; circus	das Varieté; der Zirkus
ballet; concert	das Ballett; das Konzert
dance hall; ball room	das Tanzlokal; der Ballsaal
box office; ticket	die Kasse; die Eintrittskarte, -n
seat; to book a ...	der Platz; einen Platz reservieren
a box; orchestra stalls	eine Loge; der Orchestersitz, -e
the stalls; the dress circle	das Parkett; der erste Rang
a seat in the stalls	ein Parkettplatz, ⸚e
a seat in a box	ein Logenplatz, ⸚e
three seats in the upper circle	zwei Plätze im zweiten Rang
standing room in the gallery	ein Stehplatz in der Gallerie

SPORT, AMUSEMENTS, PASTIMES

programme; opera glasses	das Programm; das Opernglas, ¨er
performance; interval	die Vorstellung; die Pause, -n
afternoon-, evening performance	die Nachmittags-, die Abendvorstellung
the stage; the play	die Bühne; das Theaterstück
comedy; tragedy	das Lustspiel; das Trauerspiel
feature film	der Hauptfilm
orchestra; conductor	das Orchester; der Dirigent
a waltz; a tango	ein Walzer; ein Tango
May I have the next dance, please?	Darf ich um den nächsten Tanz bitten?

Pastimes
Do you play . . . ?
    the piano
    the violin
    the flute
    the guitar
    chess

Zeitvertreib
Spielen Sie . . . ?
    Klavier
    Violine
    Flöte
    Gitarre
    Schach

draughts	Dame
billiards	Billiard
dominoes	Domino
cards	Karten
Are you interested in . . . ?	Haben Sie Interesse für . . . ?
painting	Malerei
sculpture	Bildhauerei
drawing	Zeichnen
architecture	Architektur
music	Musik
literature	Literatur
history	Geschichte
astronomy	Astronomie
the gramophone	das Grammophon
record player	der Plattenspieler
gramophone record	die Grammophonplatte, -n
long playing record	die Langspielplatte, -n
stereo recording	Stereo-Aufnahme
hi-fi amplifier	Hi-Fi-Verstärker
'woofer'	Tieftonlautsprecher

SPORT, AMUSEMENTS, PASTIMES

'tweeter'	Hochtonlautsprecher
to adjust	richtig einstellen
tape recorder	der Tonbrandgerät, -e
recording tape	das Tonband, ⸚er
radio set	der Radioapparat
television	das Fernsehen
television set	der Fernsehapparat
to switch on, -off	ein-, ausschalten
to listen	hören
to look	anschauen

LETTER WRITING

The Date

Berlin, den 17.11.19xx

The date is written on the top right hand side of the page and preceded by the name of the place you write from.

The month is indicated either in figures or in letters. The following abbreviations may be used: Jan., Feb., Aug., Sept., Okt., Nov., Dez. The other months which have shorter names, are not abbreviated.

The Address   *Herrn*

   Hans Müller

   <u>*München*</u>
   <u>*Jahnstrasse 28*</u>

Herrn, which is slightly raised before the name, is replaced by *Frau* or *Fräulein*, when writing to a woman, and by Herren when addressing a firm, but this is usually omitted before impersonal names, such as *Die Westdeutsche Kreditgesellschaft*.

Gesellschaft means company and the abbreviation for a limited liability company is *GmbH*, which stands for '*Gesellschaft mit beschränkter Haftung*'.

Note that the line below the name is left blank.

The Opening

(to strangers): *Sehr geehrter Herr!*
Sehr geehrte, gnädige Frau!
Sehr geehrtes, gnädiges Fräulein!

(to a firm):   *Sehr geehrte Herren!*

The latter is often omitted in regular routine correspondence between two business houses.

When the correspondents have written to each other before, or after they have met, it is customary to use their name and to write:

Sehr geehrter Herr Hartmann!
Sehr geehrte Frau Schulz!
Sehr geehrtes Fräulein Meier!

LETTER WRITING

After further acquaintance these formal salutations may be replaced by the:

(moderately familiar): *Lieber Herr Hartmann!*
Liebe Frau Schulz!
Liebes Fräulein Meier!

or (very familiar): *Lieber Hans!*
Liebe Gertrud!

The Ending

(in business letters and when writing to strangers) — *Mit ausgezeichneter Hochachtung!**
or *Mit vorzüglicher Hochachtung!**
or *Hochachtungsvoll!**

(in letters starting with any of the above salutations using the person's surname) — *Mit besten Grüßen,*
Ihr sehr ergebener* (from a man)
or *Ihre sehr ergebene** (from a woman)

*followed by the writer's signature.

(in letters starting with a salutation using the person's Christian name)	*Mit herzlichen Grüßen,* *Ihr** (from a man) *Ihre** (from a woman)
(between intimate friends who address each other as *Du* or between near relatives, or when writing to children)	*Mit vielen Grüßen (und Küssen)*** *Dein** (from a man) *Deine** (from a woman)

The address

The address on the envelope is given in the same form as inside the letter and it is customary to write the sender's address at the back of the envelope preceded by the word *Absender*:

The following indications may be used:

Postlagernd, to be called for
Dringend, urgent
per Luftpost, by airmail
per Einschreiben, registered

**and kisses.

Drucksache, printed matter
Muster ohne Wert, sample without value
Nachnahme, cash on delivery
Vertraulich, confidential
Persönlich, personal
bitte nachsenden, please forward
falls unbestellbar, bitte zurück, please return if gone away

USEFUL LETTERS FOR THE TOURIST

(1) *Letter to a tourist office asking for information*

Walton-on-Thames, 21 März 19xx

An den Verkehrsverein
Seefeld in Tirol
Österreich

Sehr geehrte Herren!

Ich beabsichtige mit meiner Familie die Sommerferien in Österreich zu verbringen und bitte Sie, mir einen Prospekt über Ihren Ort sowie eine Liste der von Ihnen empfohlenen Hotels (Pensionen, Zimmer) mit Preisangaben zu übersenden.

Ich lege einen internationalen Portoschein bei.

Ich danke Ihnen im voraus für Ihre Auskünfte.

Hochachtungsvoll,

Translation:

Dear Sirs,

I intend to spend my summer holidays with my family in Austria, and should be glad if you would send me a prospectus of your locality together with a list of recommended hotels (boarding houses, rooms) indicating their prices.

I am enclosing an international reply coupon.

Thank you in advance for your information.

                          Yours faithfully,

(2) *Letter to a local tourist office asking about camping and bathing facilities*

Sehr geehrte Herren!

Ich möchte mich erkundigen, ob es in Ihrem Ort oder in der Nähe einen Zeltlagerplatz (einen Lagerplatz für Wohnwagen) gibt. Besteht die Möglichkeit, dort ein Zelt (einen Wohnwagen) zu mieten?

Falls es solche Möglichkeiten bei Ihnen gibt, wäre ich für nähere Angaben dankbar, besonders wie weit die Entfernung zum nächsten Ort ist und ob es im Lager Wasch- und Kochgelegenheit gibt. Auch würde mich interessieren, ob es in der Nähe ein Schwimmbad gibt.

Ich lege einen internationalen Portoschein bei und danke Ihnen im voraus für Ihre Auskünfte.

                                              Hochachtungsvoll,

Translation:

Dear Sirs,

I wish to enquire whether there is in your locality or its neighbourhood a camping site (caravan site)? Would it be possible to hire a tent (a caravan) there?

If there are such facilities, I should be grateful for further particulars, especially what the distance is to the nearest town or village, and if the camp has washing and cooking facilities. I should also be interested to know whether there is a swimming bath in the neighbourhood.

I enclose an international reply coupon and thank you in anticipation for your information.

                        Yours faithfully,

(3) To the proprietor of a hotel asking if accommodation is available on a certain date

Sehr geehrter Herr!

    Meine Frau und ich beabsichtigen einige Tage in Domstadt zu verbringen und dort am 15ten Juni einzutreffen. Ich bitte Sie mir mitzuteilen, ob Sie uns unterbringen können. Geben Sie uns, bitte, Ihren Pauschalpreis mit Vollpension, sowie Ihren Preis für Halbpension an.

                                        Hochachtungsvoll,

USEFUL LETTERS FOR THE TOURIST

Translation:

Dear Sir,

My wife and I intend to spend a few days at Domstadt, arriving on the 15th of June. I shall be glad to know if you can accommodate us. Please also let me know your inclusive terms for full board, also your terms for bed and breakfast only.

Yours faithfully,

(4) *Reservation of a hotel room*

Hotel Glockenturm
Domstadt

Ich danke Ihnen für Ihr Schreiben vom 18ten ds. Mts., in dem Sie mir mitteilen, daß Sie mir ein Doppelzimmer für die Zeit vom 15ten bis 21sten Juni zur Verfügung stellen können.

Ich ersehe aus der beigelegten Preisliste, daß der Preis für ein Doppelzimmer mit Bad einschließlich Frühstück 50 DM pro Tag beträgt und bitte Sie, mir das Zimmer zu diesen Bedingungen zu reservieren.

Wir werden am 15ten Juni in den Abendstunden eintreffen.

Translation:

I thank you for your letter of the 18th inst., telling me that you could reserve me a double room for the period 15th to 21st of June.

I see from the price-list you enclosed, that you charge 50 DM for a double room with bath, breakfast included, and should be glad if you would reserve me a room at these terms.

We shall arrive on the 15th of June towards the evening.

(5) To the proprietress of a boarding house

Sehr geehrte Frau Lachner!

Ihre Pension ist uns vom dortigen Verkehrsverein (von Familie Smith, die letztes Jahr bei Ihnen war) empfohlen worden.

Wir würden gerne dieses Jahr zu Ihnen kommen und zwar für drei Wochen, vom 8ten bis zum 28ten August. Sollte es Ihnen nicht möglich sein, uns für diese Zeit unterzubringen, könnten wir unsere Ferien um eine bis zwei Wochen verschieben.

Unsere Familie besteht außer meiner Frau und mir aus vier Kindern im Alter von 15, 12, 8 und 5 Jahren. Zwei Zimmer würden uns genügen. Ein Kind könnte bei uns schlafen und die anderen in einem Zimmer mit drei Betten.

Sollte es Ihnen möglich sein, uns zu der angegebenen Zeit unterzubringen, wäre ich Ihnen für baldige Mitteilung mit Angabe des Pauschalpreises für die ganze Familie sehr dankbar.

Mit vorzüglicher Hochachtung,

USEFUL LETTERS FOR THE TOURIST

Translation:

Your boarding house has been recommended to us by the tourist office in your town (by the Smith family who stayed with you last year). We should like to stay with you this year for three weeks from the 8th to the 28th of August. Should you not be able to accommodate us for this period, we could postpone our holidays by one to two weeks. Besides myself and my wife, our family consists of four children, aged 15, 12, 8 and 5. Two rooms should be sufficient. One child could sleep with us and the others share a room with three beds. Should you be able to accommodate us during the period stated, I would be grateful for an early reply, stating your inclusive terms for the whole family.

                      Yours faithfully,

(6) *To a seaside landlady*

Sehr geehrte Frau Bauer!

Ich entnehme Ihre Adresse einer mir vom dortigen Verkehrsbüro übersandten Liste von Zimmervermietern und bitte Sie, mir mitzuteilen, ob Sie für die Zeit vom 1sten bis 14ten Juli Zimmer frei haben.

Es handelt sich um meine Freundin und mich, und wir würden zwei Einzelzimmer vorziehen. Falls es nicht anders geht, könnten wir uns mit einem Zimmer mit zwei Einzelbetten begnügen.

Sollten Sie uns für diese Zeit unterbringen können, bitten wir, außer der Preisangabe, uns mitzuteilen ob die Zimmer Fließwasser haben und auch, ob man bei Ihnen Frühstück und eventuell andere Mahlzeiten haben kann.

Wie weit ist das Haus von der See entfernt? Gibt es gute, aber nicht zu teure Restaurants in nicht zu großer Entfernung?

Mit bestem Dank in Voraus für Beantwortung meiner Anfrage

        Hochachtungsvoll!

USEFUL LETTERS FOR THE TOURIST

Translation:

Dear Mrs Bauer,

I obtained your address from a list of furnished rooms supplied by the tourist office in your locality and should be glad to know whether you have a vacancy for the fortnight from the 1st to the 14th of July.

We are two friends who would prefer separate rooms, but if you cannot provide these, would also consider one room with two separate beds.

If you could accommodate us during this period, I should be glad to know whether the rooms have running hot and cold water and also whether you provide breakfast and other meals.

How far is your house from the sea? Are there any good, but not too expensive restaurants in reasonable distance?

Thanking you in anticipation of your kind reply,

Yours faithfully,

(7) *To an estate agent enquiring about a villa*

Herren Masius & Co.
    Haus—und Wohnungsagentur

Schönbad
Wilhelmstrasse 33

Sehr geehrte Herren!

    Wir wünschen eine Villa in Schönbad oder in der Nähe des Ortes für die Zeit vom 1sten Juli bis 30sten September zu mieten.

    Sie soll vollständig möbliert sein und ein bis zwei Badezimmer enthalten, sowie Schlafgelegenheit für neun Personen, zwei Ehepaare, die jedes ein eigenes Schlafzimmer benötigen. Die anderen sind Kinder, die gemeinsam schlafen können. Eines könnte nötigenfalls auf dem Sofa im Wohnzimmer schlafen.

    Ich bitte, mir eine Liste geeigneter Villen zu übersenden mit genauer Angabe ihrer Lage und, falls möglich, mit Photographien derselben.

                      In Erwartung Ihrer baldigen Nachricht,
                           Hochachtungsvoll!

USEFUL LETTERS FOR THE TOURIST

Translation:

Dear Sirs,

We wish to rent a villa at or near Schönbad from the 1st of July until the end of September.

It would have to be fully furnished and contain one or two bathrooms, as well as sleeping accommodation for nine: two married couples requiring a bedroom each and five children who could share rooms. One child could, if necessary, sleep on the living room couch.

I should be glad to have a list of suitable villas with indications of their exact location and preferably accompanied by photographs.

Trusting to hear from you soon,

                              Yours faithfully,

(8) *Reservation of rooms (in reply to (5))*

Sehr geehrte Frau Lachner!

Ich bestätige Ihr Schreiben vom 29 v.Mts. und danke Ihnen für Ihre Angaben.

Ich freue mich, daß Sie uns unterbringen können und bitte, uns die beiden Zimmer zu den angegebenen Bedingungen reservieren zu wollen.

Ich nehme an, daß beide Zimmer Fließwasser haben und daß der Pauschalpreis von 70 Schweizer Franken pro Tag Bedienung sowie alle weiteren Abgaben einschließt.

Mit der Bitte, mir die Reservation bestätigen zu wollen, verbleibe ich,

Ihr sehr ergebener,

USEFUL LETTERS FOR THE TOURIST

Translation:

Dear Mrs Lachner,

I thank you for your letter of the 29th ult.

I am glad that you are able to accommodate us and should be glad if you would reserve the two rooms for us at the terms stated in your letter.

I assume that both rooms have hot and cold running water, and that the inclusive price of 70 Swiss Francs per day includes service and all further charges.

I should be glad if you would kindly confirm this reservation, and remain,

        Yours very truly,

(9) *Request for confirmation*

Sehr geehrte Frau Lachner!

Ich schrieb Ihnen am 2ten ds. Mts. und bat Sie, die mir in Ihrem Schreiben vom 29ten v. Mts. angebotenen zwei Zimmer zu reservieren Auch bat ich um Bestätigung dieser Reservation.

Da ich diese bisher nicht erhalten habe, gestatte ich mir anzufragen, ob Sie mein Schreiben erhalten haben und die Reservation der beiden Zimmer in Ordnung ist.

In Erwartung Ihrer umgehenden Antwort, verbleibe ich,

Ihr sehr ergebener,

Translation:

Dear Mrs. Lachner,

I wrote to you on the 2nd inst. asking you to reserve for me the two rooms offered to me in your letter of the 29th ult. I also asked you to kindly confirm this reservation.

As I have not heard from you, I wish to enquire whether you received my letter and whether the reservation has been made.

Awaiting your immediate reply, I remain,

                        Yours very truly,

(10) *Cancellation of a reservation*

Am 3ten ds.Mts. bat ich Sie, mir ein Zimmer vom 25ten Mai ab reservieren zu wollen. Sie bestätigten diese Reservation mit Ihrem Schreiben vom 7ten ds. Mts.

Ich muß Sie leider bitten, diese Reservation rückgängig zu machen, da ich unvorhergesehener Umstände halber die Reise auf unbestimmte Zeit verschieben muß.

USEFUL LETTERS FOR THE TOURIST

Translation:

On the 3rd of the month I asked you to reserve for me a room from the 25th of May. You confirmed this reservation in your letter of the 7th inst. Unfortunately I have to request you to cancel this reservation, as in view of unforeseen circumstances I have to postpone the journey indefinitely.

Appendix

COUNTRIES, THEIR LANGUAGES AND INHABITANTS

Name of Country	Corresponding Adjective or Language	Inhabitant[1]
Africa—Afrika	afrikanisch	Afrikaner
America—Amerika	amerikanisch	Amerikaner
Arabia—Arabien	arabisch	Araber
Argentina—Argentinien	argentinisch	Argentinier
Asia—Asien	asiatisch	Asiat
Austria—Oesterreich	österreichisch	Oesterreicher
Bavaria—Bayern	bayrisch	Bayer

Name of Country	Corresponding Adjective or Language	Inhabitant[1]
Brazil—Brasilien	brasilianisch	Brasilianer
Belgium—Belgien	belgisch	Belgier
Great Britain—Großbritannien	britisch	Brite
Canada—Kanada	kanadisch	Kanadier
Chile—Chile	chilenisch	Chilene
China—China	chinesisch	Chinese
Czechoslovakia	die Tschechoslowakei	Tscheche
Denmark—Dänemark	dänisch	Däne
Egypt	ägyptisch	Aegypter
England—England	englisch	Engländer
Europe—Europa	europäisch	Europäer
Finland—Finnland	finnisch	Finne
France—Frankreich	französisch	Franzose
Germany—Deutschland	deutsch	Deutscher[2]
Greece—Griechenland	griechisch	Grieche
Holland—Holland	holländisch	Holländer
Hungary—Ungarn	ungarisch	Ungar

COUNTRIES, THEIR LANGUAGES AND INHABITANTS

Name of Country	Corresponding Adjective or Language	Inhabitant
India—Indien	indisch	Inder
Ireland—Irland	irisch	Ire
Israel—Israel	israelisch	Israeli
Japan—Japan	japanisch	Japaner
Mexico—Mexiko	mexikanisch	Mexikaner
New Zealand—Neuseeland	neuseeländisch	Neuseeländer
Norway—Norwegen	norwegisch	Norweger
Pakistan—Pakistan	pakistanisch	Pakistaner
Poland—Polen	polnisch	Pole
Portugal—Portugal	portugiesisch	Portugiese
Russia—Russland	russisch	Russe
Scotland—Schottland	schottisch	Schotte
South Africa—Südafrika	südafrikanisch	Südafrikaner
South America—Südamerika	südamerikanisch	Südamerikaner
Spain—Spanien	spanisch	Spanier
Sweden—Schweden	schwedisch	Schwede

Name of Country	Corresponding Adjective or Language	Inhabitant
Switzerland— die Schweiz	schweizer	Schweizer
Turkey—die Türkei	türkisch	Türke
U.S.A.—die Vereinigten Staaten	amerikanisch	Amerikaner
Wales—Wales	waliesisch	Walieser
Yugoslavia— Jugoslawien	jugoslawisch	Jugoslawe

NOTE

[1] The forms given are the masculine forms, singular. For the feminine singular, add -in to the masculine form, *e.g.* the English women = die Engländerin. Where the masculine form ends in "e" it is dropped and "in" added, *e.g.* der Russe = the Russian (man); die Russin = the Russian (woman). The plural of the masculine form in -er remains unchanged: der Afrikaner = the African, die Afrikaner = the Africans. The nouns

ending in -e add "n" in Plural: der Pole = the Pole, die Polen = the Poles. The feminines double the final n and add -in: die Engländerinnen = the English women.

[2] The German woman is die Deutsche. The Germans (men and women) = die Deutschen; a German = ein Deutscher; a German woman = eine Deutsche.

Western Germany, die Deutsche Bundesrepublik.

Eastern Germany, die Deutsche Demokratische Republik.

EMERGENCIES AND ACCIDENTS

(for non-urgent illnesses and other aspects of the Human body see pages 170 to 175)

Emergency	Notfall
illness	Krankheit
heart attack	Herzanfall
he has collapsed	er ist zusammengebrochen
appendicitis	Blinddarmentzündung
he has stopped breathing	er atmet nicht mehr
he has fainted	er ist ohnmächtig
he has been poisoned with this	er hat sich hiermit vergiftet
he has taken an overdose of this	er hat eine Überdosis hiervon genommen
he has a high temperature	er hat hohes Fieber
the baby is arriving	Die Geburt steht bevor
he is having a fit	er hat einen Anfall

EMERGENCIES AND ACCIDENTS

Accidents	Unfälle
there has been an accident	es ist ein Unfall passiert
the car has crashed	es ist ein Verkehrsunfall passiert
plane	Flugzeugunglück
train	Zugunglück
he has been seriously injured	er ist schwerverletzt
he has broken his arm (leg)	er hat sich den Arm (das Bein) gebrochen
he is unconscious	er ist bewusstlos
he is being swept away to sea	er wird von der Flut mitgerissen
he is drowning	er ertrinkt
the boat has capsized	das Boot ist gekentert
man overboard!	Mann über Bord
he has been attacked (robbed)	er wurde überfallen (beraubt)
he has fallen down the mountain (cliff)	er ist vom Berg (von der Klippe) abgestürzt
there has been an avalanche	eine Lawine ist heruntergekommen
he has had an electric shock	er hat einen elektrischen Schock erlitten

CALLING FOR HELP

Please will you call for help	Bitte rufen Sie Hilfe herbei
a doctor	einen Arzt
an ambulance	einen Krankenwagen
the coastguards	die Küstenwache
the fire brigade	die Feuewehr
Please call out a rescue party	Bitte besorgen Sie eine Rettungsmannshaft
Please call out the air-sea rescue	Bitte rufen Sie den Luft-See Rettungsdienst

Telephones in Germany are marked NOTRUF and the appropriate number of the emergency service.

THE SUNSHINE PHRASE BOOKS

Uniform with this book

Sunshine German Phrase Book
Sunshine French Phrase Book
Sunshine Italian Phrase Book
Sunshine Spanish Phrase Book

Some paperfronts are listed on the following pages. A full list of the titles currently available can be had by sending a stamped addressed envelope to:

Elliot Right Way Books, Lower Kingswood, Tadworth, Surrey, U.K.

Some other Paperfronts:

Healthy Houseplants A−Z
Out Of The Freezer Into The Microwave
Microwave Cooking Properly Explained
Food Processors Properly Explained
Slow Cooking Properly Explained
Wine Making The Natural Way
Easymade Wine
Traditional Beer And Cider Making
Handbook Of Herbs
Buying Or Selling A House

Elliot Right Way Books, Kingswood, Surrey, U.K.

Some other Paperfronts:

Highway Code Questions And Answers
Car Driving In Two Weeks
Learning To Drive In Pictures
Pass Your Motor-cycle L Test
Car Repairs Properly Explained
Car Doctor A–Z
Begin Chess
Right Way To Play Chess
Begin Bridge
The Knot Book

Elliot Right Way Books, Kingswood, Surrey, U.K.

Some other Paperfronts:

How To Have A Well-Mannered Dog
Right Way To Keep Dogs
Right Way To Keep Pet Fish
Babies Names A–Z
Your Business – Right Way To Run It
Book-Keeping The Right Way
Business Letters
Wedding Etiquette Properly Explained
Best Man's Duties
Sample Social Speeches

Elliot Right Way Books, Kingswood, Surrey, U.K.